THE HUMAN
ENTERPRISE

About the Book and Author

The Human Enterprise presents a wide-ranging but well-integrated analysis of contemporary anthropological theory. The author explains clearly and cogently how to evaluate scientific theories and encourages students to think critically about the nature of theory itself. Thoughtful and thought-provoking, this text should be a stimulating addition to courses on anthropological theory.

Part One examines the philosophical foundations of anthropological theory, with particular attention to the nature of scientific inquiry and the mechanisms of scientific progress. The author proposes an original approach to the comparison and evaluation of competing scientific paradigms. Part Two explores the nature of social science and describes distinctive features of anthropology such as the concept of culture and the emic/etic distinction.

The author then surveys the range of research strategies employed by anthropologists and presents a detailed analysis of cultural materialism, structuralism, and symbolic anthropology. The final section uses two celebrated issues—the argument about the image of limited good and the sacred cow controversy—to illustrate the current nature of paradigmatic debate and to indicate how a clearer understanding of the nature of paradigms and theory might resolve such controversies.

James Lett has taught anthropology and philosophy at the University of Florida, Barry University, and the Florida Institute of Technology. He currently teaches at Indian River Community College.

THE HUMAN ENTERPRISE

A Critical Introduction to Anthropological Theory

James Lett

Westview Press / Boulder and London

Copyright © 1987 by Westview Press, Inc.

Published in 1987 in the United States of America by Westview Press, Inc.; Frederick A. Praeger, Publisher; 5500 Central Avenue, Boulder, Colorado 80301

Library of Congress Cataloging-in-Publication Data
Lett, James W.
   The human enterprise.
   Includes index.
   1. Anthropology—Philosophy.   2. Anthropology—
Methodology.   I. Title.
GN33.L38   1987   306′.01   86-28987
ISBN 0-8133-0421-0
ISBN 0-8133-0422-9 (pbk.)

Printed and bound in the United States of America

The paper used in this publication meets the requirements of the American National Standard for Permanence of Paper for Printed Library Materials Z39.48-1984.

10   9   8   7   6   5   4   3   2   1

Science and philosophy are different kinds of intellectual activity, yet both are concerned with explaining the world. If in the long run they do not complement each other, the human enterprise will suffer.
—*Reuben Abel,*
Man Is the Measure

Contents

Acknowledgments

Writing this book has been a pleasant task, thanks in no small part to the generous support and assistance of a sizable number of talented and exceptional people, including Holly Arrow, Karen Bryant, David Hosley, Suzanne Hutcheson, Dani Lee, Richard Schneider, Judith Stifel, Vicki Turner, and Gayle Yamada. I want to specifically acknowledge my debt, however, to five anthropologists who have had a profound influence upon my thinking. All have contributed their wisdom to this book; all have read it at least once in one version or another; none agrees with all of my conclusions. I am grateful to all five.

Dr. Nathan Altshuler, of the College of William and Mary, first inspired my interest in anthropological theory in the fall of 1976. I recognized his remarkable insight at the time, but I had to learn much more about the discipline and the world before I truly appreciated his brilliance. Most of what I know about the philosophical approach to anthropological theory I learned from him.

Much of the rest of what I know about anthropological theory I learned from Dr. Marvin Harris at the University of Florida. I disagree with him on several points (although I will let him speak for himself— he is more than capable of defending his own position), but I know of no other contemporary anthropologist who has responded to the challenge of theory more courageously or more creatively. He has my abiding respect and my sincere thanks.

My decision to become an anthropologist and my decision to pursue graduate studies at the University of Florida were influenced strongly by Dr. Charles Wagley. The model of his scholarship and his writing attracted me to the discipline in the first place, and the example of his personal fortitude (eloquently recalled in his remarkable ethnography, *Welcome of Tears*) sustained me during my first lengthy fieldwork experience. If there is anything in contemporary U.S. anthropology that is likely to stand the test of time, to be read and appreciated years from now for something other than its historical value, it is to be found in the sensitive, poignant, lyrical writings of Loren Eiseley and Charles Wagley.

This book has undergone several major revisions since its original conception in the fall of 1982, and at each stage I have benefited substantially from the patient and perceptive criticism of Dr. Robert Lawless at the University of Florida. I have relied frequently on his exceptional command of the anthropological literature and his keen ability to discern subtle errors of logic and interpretation. Whatever balance this book contains is due chiefly to his efforts.

Finally, I owe an inestimable personal and professional debt to the chairperson of my doctoral committee at the University of Florida, Dr. Theron Nunez. Throughout my career, he has been a constant source of unerringly good advice and uncommonly resourceful support. He is the person primarily responsible for having shaped my vision of anthropology, and the influence of his extraordinary intellect is amply evident in these pages. As I write this, he is battling cancer with the same courage, honesty, and inimitable style that have marked his entire life. This book is dedicated to him with affection and appreciation.

James Lett

Prologue:
The Challenge of Theory

All order, I've come to understand,
is theoretical, unreal—a harmless, sensible,
smiling mask men slide between the two great,
dark realities, the self and the world.
—John Gardner, Grendel

This is a book about theory in sociocultural anthropology, although it is not a history of anthropological thought, nor is it a catalog of the many anthropological theories in vogue today. Instead, this book is about the philosophical foundations of anthropological theory. My aim is to describe the basic building blocks of theory and to lay out the essential architectural principles of paradigm construction. I do not offer a blueprint for a particular theoretical edifice (although I do not hesitate to point out the designs that I consider to be most promising)—instead, I try to identify what seem to me to be the essential engineering requisites for sound theoretical structures.

This is, then, an abstract book, but I have tried to make it as practical and down-to-earth as possible. I analyze particular anthropological paradigms in some detail, and I have included specific concrete illustrations wherever I could. The purpose of this book, however, is not to persuade you to adopt a particular theoretical perspective, or to provide you with a comprehensive survey of anthropological theories, but to teach you to think clearly about the nature of theory itself and then to show you how to apply that lesson to any and all theories you might encounter in the pursuit of the anthropological enterprise. I have

1

tried to write a deliberately provocative book; my pedagogical purpose will be served if I can inspire you to critical reflection.

This book contains a good deal more philosophical analysis than most textbooks on anthropological theory, but I hope to show that anthropology could benefit from a good deal more philosophical attention. I realize, however, that many anthropologists are likely to think otherwise. I have never understood why the discipline of philosophy is popularly perceived as a puzzling and even pointless activity, because philosophy is nothing more than an unwavering commitment to clarity of thought, precision of expression, and validity of inference. Put even more simply, philosophical analysis is nothing more than an attempt to ensure that we mean what we say and say what we mean. Obviously, then, scientists can ill afford to avoid such analysis, yet it is unfortunately true, as anthropologist Bob Scholte (1980:72) observes, that "the philosophical context of anthropological *praxis* has never been a major concern of ethnographers and ethnologists." I agree with Reuben Abel (1976:xxiii) that "it is stultifying for the scientist to ignore the logical analysis of his [or her] concepts and suppositions," and that is why I have written this book.

In the final analysis, this entire book turns on a single philosophical problem, one that lies at the heart of the human predicament: namely, the dilemma of epistemology. All debates, all controversies, all questions of fact or value are ultimately reducible to the question of knowledge: How do we know what we know? The one great lesson of epistemology is that knowledge is notoriously problematic. Even the information provided by our five senses is variable, subjective, and sometimes misleading. Our perceptions of the external world are necessarily selective. Our frames of reference are molded by context, experience, and pre-disposition. The range of our perceptions is restricted by the limits of our sensory apparatus. Perception requires active, although usually not deliberate, interpretation.

There is an irreducibly human dimension to all that is knowable, for it is impossible to describe the really real except in human terms. What is real is determined by the idiosyncracies of human perception and cognition. Our understanding of the world is founded upon the concepts we form and hold about the world, but those concepts are forged in the crucible of human experience. Our taxonomies, our interpretations, and even our perceptions are variable products of our intellects. They are not dictated by the real or true nature of the world itself, whatever that might be. This is what philosophers mean when they say there is a "loose fit between the mind and the world."

Knowledge, in short, depends upon theories, the variably implicit and explicit frameworks for interpretation that shape our perceptions, guide our judgments, color our analyses, and influence our beliefs. In popular usage, *fact* and *theory* refer to fundamentally different sorts of things. Facts are assumed to have an independent, objective existence. They are thought to be the immutable bits and pieces of objective reality. Theories, on the other hand, are regarded as hypothetical abstractions, unproven or even incorrect suppositions about the nature and relationships of facts. In everyday parlance, a fact is a fact, but a theory is often "just a theory."

In actuality, however, facts do not exist apart from theories. Facts are determined by the instruments (whether human or artificial) used to measure them. Sapir and Whorf have suggested that the perception of facts is influenced by the language of the observer. The identification of facts unquestionably is conditioned by the influence of culture, but, most importantly, facts are determined by the theories that define their existence. For example, the "fact" that most archeological sites are composed of various strata representing different periods of occupation is a "fact" that is determined by the theory of stratigraphy. Those who are unaware of the theory, such as pothunters or graverobbers, will fail to perceive and appreciate the facts. (Whether a site is looted or excavated, however, it is still destroyed, and that creates a disturbing problem for professional archeologists. What "facts" that might have been illuminated by tomorrow's theories are being destroyed by today's digging?) The point is that *theoretical* and *unreal* are not synonymous terms. There is no *atheoretical* way to describe and understand reality.

Because many of our theories are implicit—perhaps even unknowable—there is a significant tacit component to our knowledge of the world. Do you know what it is about your friend's voice that makes it recognizable on the telephone? Can you describe the fragrance of your favorite cologne? How do you arrive at aesthetic judgments? What is creativity? How does the imagination work? This is what Michael Polanyi (1966:4) means when he says "we know more than we can tell." Knowledge is elusive; absolute certainty is, perhaps, logically unattainable.

Despite all this, it would be a severe mistake to embrace the notion that no reliable knowledge is possible. It would be similarly indefensible to conclude that all knowledge is relative. The barriers to knowledge are practical, not logical. Our ability to predict and control empirical phenomena demonstrates that our knowledge of the world is more than mere illusion. Indeed, the so-called "pragmatic" perspectives offer the best solution to the philosophical problem of truth. A true proposition is one that consistently and reliably satisfies our desire and need to perceive, understand, predict, and control the world.

This does not mean, incidentally, that what is expedient is true. Although it may be useful at times to believe false statements (for example, to accept your own rationalizations), the pragmatic criteria for truth are not so easily satisfied. What is established as true on pragmatic grounds must be true for all people in all places in all times. A true proposition must be consistently and universally true. (For a philosophical analysis of the nature of truth, see Hospers 1967:114–121.)

This, then, is the challenge of theory: to tailor the loose fit between the mind and the world; to be aware of the limits of perception; to recognize the pervasive significance of theory; to develop standards of proof and disproof; to specify the criteria for belief; to examine our presuppositions and assumptions; to make our hypotheses as comprehensive, consistent, and reliable as possible; to accept the implications of contradiction and to abandon those beliefs that have been contradicted; to critically evaluate competing accounts of the world; to make our knowledge of the world as certain and self-correcting as possible; in short, to see beyond the "smiling mask of order" to the "dark reality of the world." The challenge of theory is the challenge of responsible inquiry.

The domain of possible inquiry is infinitely large, but the one problem that has never failed to beguile human beings is the puzzle of the human condition. Who are we? How did we come to be? What are the reasons and purposes and consequences for and of our lives and our actions? What does it all mean? The human condition is the anthropological domain of inquiry.

Throughout this book, I am concerned with a single theme: What would responsible inquiry into the human condition entail? I argue for a particular perspective on anthropological knowledge: What we know about the human condition is fundamentally dependent, in the fullest sense, upon how we know what we know. That premise underlies my analysis of scientific progress and its mechanisms and forms the basis of my evaluation of competing anthropological paradigms.

I start with the broadest possible questions. What is knowledge? How can we achieve certainty? What is science? What do we mean by explanation? How does scientific knowledge grow and develop? These questions are addressed in Part One, which is concerned with epistemology and related issues in the philosophy of science.

Next I consider what a social science should be. Is it possible to conduct a scientific inquiry into the human condition? If so, what aspects of the human condition require explanation? What would constitute an adequate explanation of the human experience? These issues are considered in Part Two, which examines the essential features of the anthropological approach to the study of humanity.

Then I look at the ongoing process of theory building in contemporary anthropology. Which paradigms or research strategies are favored among anthropologists today? Which of the extant paradigms best satisfies the criteria of responsible inquiry? To which contemporary paradigm should anthropologists commit themselves? These questions are examined in Part Three, which is devoted to a review and analysis of contemporary anthropological theory.

Finally, I focus attention upon the conduct of anthropological research and analysis. How adept are anthropologists at the recognition and analysis of paradigmatic issues? How effectively are paradigmatic differences communicated and debated? What are the criteria by which anthropologists accept or reject rival paradigms? These questions are considered in Part Four, which examines the nature of paradigmatic debate in anthropology.

My intent has been to make the arguments in this book cumulative and progressive, and I am satisfied that I have succeeded. More sophisticated readers may be tempted to skip some of the earlier chapters and jump directly to the analysis of contemporary anthropological paradigms, but be forewarned: Each chapter presumes a familiarity with the arguments found in its predecessor, and readers who gloss over some of the early conclusions may find themselves missing some of the later premises.

PART ONE

THE PHILOSOPHY OF SCIENCE

I do not believe in Belief.
—E. M. Forster,
"What I Believe"

1

The Pursuit
of Knowledge

First things first. This book is devoted to a critical analysis of the nature, meaning, implications, and significance of anthropological theory—in other words, to a philosophical analysis of anthropological thought. However, this book is not addressed to philosophers; instead, it is intended for those who wish to study anthropology and as such presumes no intimate acquaintance with the discipline of philosophy. Readers who have had prior exposure to the methods of philosophical analysis may enjoy some slight advantage, but I suspect that there are very few students who are not at least intuitively acquainted with the philosophical approach. For those students who would be more comfortable with a more formal introduction, however, I will say a word or two about philosophical analysis.

The essential activity of philosophy is the construction and critical appraisal of arguments. An argument is a set of linked statements in which the final statement, the conclusion, is claimed to be derived from the preceding statements, the premises. Philosophers say an argument is *valid* if the conclusion follows unavoidably from the premises; an argument is said to be *sound* if it is valid and if its premises are true. The conclusion of a sound argument is a *true* conclusion.

A sound argument, then, is by definition valid; a valid argument is not necessarily sound. Consider this argument, for example: Prolonged confinement to small crowded dwellings during an arctic winter always induces *pibloktoq* (the culturally patterned mental disorder found among the Eskimo, which manifests itself in hysterical behavior and convulsive movements); Quertilig was confined to a small crowded dwelling for the entire winter; therefore Quertilig developed *pibloktoq*. The argument is valid; its conclusion does follow unavoidably from its premises. If prolonged confinement always causes *pibloktoq* and if Quertilig was confined for a prolonged period of time, then she must have developed *pibloktoq*. However, the argument is not sound, because the first premise is untrue. Prolonged confinement does not always cause *pibloktoq*. The conclusion cannot thus be established from the argument (even though it may be true that Quertilig is in fact suffering from *pibloktoq*). Conversely, consider this example: Prolonged confinement sometimes causes *pibloktoq*; Quertilig was confined for a prolonged period of time; therefore she developed *pibloktoq*. That argument is not valid because the conclusion does not follow unavoidably from the premises. If prolonged confinement causes *pibloktoq* only sometimes, then sometimes it does not—and being invalid, the argument also is unsound. Soundness and validity are crucial concepts in the analysis of arguments, and I will use them extensively (although usually implicitly) when critiquing anthropological arguments.

Two other philosophical terms that will be used extensively are *necessary* and *sufficient* conditions. Philosophers say that P is a *necessary* condition for Q if Q can exist only in conjunction with P. A temperature of zero degrees centigrade or less, for example, is a necessary condition for ice. We say that P is a *sufficient* condition for Q if P in and of itself always will suffice to bring about the occurrence of Q, even though Q may occur otherwise in the absence of P. Depriving an air-breathing animal of oxygen for an extended period of time, for example, always will suffice to cause the animal's death, but the animal can (and eventually will) die even if never deprived of oxygen for any length of time. The withholding of oxygen, then, is a sufficient but not necessary condition for an animal's death. (Notice that prolonged confinement is neither sufficient nor necessary for *pibloktoq*—it is not sufficient because not everyone who is confined for a prolonged period of time develops *pibloktoq*; it is not necessary because some people develop *pibloktoq* without having been confined.)

Philosophical analysis is simply a technique for discerning truth. A fundamental premise of philosophy, and of this book, is that it always is possible to distinguish between truth and falsity by rational inquiry. What I attempt to do throughout this book is to apply the standards of reasonable critique to the fundamental questions of anthropological inquiry.

The crucial question implicit in any statement about the world or anything in it is the question of epistemology, or the question of knowledge. Epistemology is one of the oldest and most important branches of philosophy and is the branch most directly relevant to our interests and concerns as anthropologists. Simply defined, epistemology is *the study of the nature and source of knowledge.* Any statement of fact is a claim to knowledge; epistemology is concerned with the validity or appropriateness of such claims. What follows is a brief review of the basics of epistemological analysis.

The Nature of Knowledge

In English, the verb *to know* has a highly ambiguous and imprecise meaning. We use it when we speak of *knowing* a person, or *knowing how* to perform a task, or *knowing what* the facts of a given situation are. Many other languages resolve this ambiguity somewhat by distinguishing between knowledge by acquaintance and knowledge about entities, events, and relationships. Thus, Latin has *cognoscere* and *scire,* French has *connaître* and *savoir,* Spanish has *conocer* and *saber,* Italian has *conoscere* and *sapere,* and German has *kennen* and *wissen.* The sense of the verb *to know* that is most directly relevant to the concerns of epistemology is the propositional sense, or the sense of knowing *what* is the case.

A propositional statement is an assertion; it makes a claim about the world that is either true or false. Many of our statements are not propositional, although they nevertheless convey information. Ethical prescriptions, for instance (such as the statement that we ought to respect a person's individual liberty), are not propositional; we may agree or disagree with them, but we cannot say that they are either true or false. Statements that express sentiment or whose intent is to persuade are often devoid of propositional content. Such statements have instead an emotive meaning, although emotive statements often are expressed in what appears to be propositional form. During the Reagan administration's first term, for example, Vice President George Bush paid an official visit to the Vatican, where he remarked that the pope has "a special understanding of the spiritual dimensions of the problem of world peace." Bush was not claiming, of course, that the pope enjoyed some special knowledge denied the rest of us; instead, what the vice president meant to communicate was that he respected the pope's moral authority, or wanted to be perceived as someone who respected the pope's moral authority in order not to offend Catholic voters, or both. Emotive utterances play an indispensable role in human life; but in scientific discourse, it is absolutely essential to distinguish between emotive and propositional statements.

This is a crucial point and one that needs amplification. Often, when emotive statements are presented in what would appear to be propositional form, it is difficult at first glance to recognize that the statement is not propositional. For example, suppose I claim to know that the vintage 1959 Chateau Mouton Rothschild is the finest wine produced anywhere in the world in this century. That would appear to be a propositional assertion; it would appear to be either true or false, and I could offer substantial evidence to convince you that it in fact is true. I could point out, for example, that the Mouton '59 possesses extraordinary qualities. I could draw your attention to the wine's opulent bouquet, exceedingly rich color, and sensuously soft, velvety finish. It is full-bodied, flavorful, and infused with the unmistakable character of a classic vintage. It has all the charm and subtlety of a great Pauillac, and yet it has a distinctive quality, a nobility, that it shares with no other wine. In short, the Mouton '59 is the epitome of the wine maker's art. That may well be a compelling argument, but it is not a propositional claim. The difficulty lies in the ambiguity and imprecision of the term "finest." What exactly does that mean? What qualities would the "finest" wine possess? Even if we specify what we believe those qualities to be, can we get everyone (or anyone) to agree with our definition? Ultimately, the claim that the Mouton '59 is the finest wine produced in this century turns out to be an emotive utterance. It is not an attempt to assert a propositional claim about the world, but an attempt to persuade you to adopt a particular set of aesthetic values.

The problem here, and the real point of this example, is that emotive utterances are all too common in the social sciences. What happens far too frequently is that particular value positions that are firmly established in popular culture are taken up by social scientists and dressed in what would appear to be propositional form and then offered as scientific assertions about the nature of the world.

For example, consider the following assertion, originally formulated by medical scientists but subsequently promulgated by social scientists: Alcoholism is a disease. The validity of that assertion is affirmed by the American Medical Association and by the many schools of psychotherapeutic practice that have been developed to deal with people who abuse chemical substances. The assumption that alcoholism is a disease is a cornerstone of the effective treatment programs administered by Alcoholics Anonymous.

The simple assertion that "alcoholism is a disease" would appear to be propositional. Whether it is true or false, of course, would depend upon the meaning of the term "disease." When most medical and social scientists say that alcoholism is a disease, they mean that alcoholism is a progressive and debilitating condition characterized by predictable symptoms that include compulsive and excessive alcohol consumption, deteriorating physical and psychological health, and social alienation. Those who assert that alcoholism is a disease believe that there is something in a person's physical makeup that makes him or her incapable of social drinking. Alcoholics are born, not made, runs the argument: One drink is sufficient to trigger the irresistible onset of potentially fatal symptoms. Physicians and psychotherapists who subscribe to the theory believe that approximately 14 percent of the people in any population are either latent or developed alcoholics.

By that definition, then, is it true that alcoholism is a disease? Are 14 percent of the people in any population genetically predisposed, for some as yet undiscovered reason, to consume alcohol uncontrollably? Perhaps so, but that claim can hardly be considered propositional. The problem arises when one attempts to define whether any given person is an alcoholic or not. How, in other words, can the "disease" of alcoholism be diagnosed? At present, there is only one way: A patient is identified as an alcoholic only (and always) if he or she is (or has been) drinking compulsively to the point where his or her physical and psychological health are deteriorating. In other words, a person is an alcoholic if he or she behaves like an alcoholic. Before people begin behaving that way, there is no physiological or psychological test that will detect the presence of the disease.

In short, the assertion that "alcoholism is a disease" may well be true, but that assertion should be regarded as a hypothesis and not as a proposition. It is, of course, usually offered as a statement of fact. There is no way, as yet, to determine whether that assertion is true or false; the evidence equally supports the hypothesis that alcoholism is simply a maladaptive pattern of behavior with no physical causes. (Who would not suffer declining physical and psychological health if he or she were to drink as much as an alcoholic drinks?) If there is no way to determine whether an assertion is true or false, then that assertion is not propositional.

In many ways, the notion that alcoholism is a disease is analogous to our culture's concept of mental illness. In both cases, the idea of "disease" is metaphorically joined to the facts of behavior and perception—and there is serious reason for questioning whether that metaphor is propositional. In several remarkably lucid books, the psychiatrist Thomas Szasz (1961; 1963; 1978) argues that the metaphor of mental illness cannot be appropriately applied to the phenomena of personal unhappiness and socially deviant behavior. In the first place, as Szasz points out in *Law, Liberty, and Psychiatry*, the concept of "mental illness"—the notion that the mind or the personality can somehow be diseased or deformed—requires us to redefine what we generally mean by "illness." "Physical illness," as Szasz (1963:17) observes, "is usually something that *happens* to us, whereas mental illness is something we *do* (or feel or think)." In the second place, the diagnosis of mental illness is not made solely with reference to objective criteria, nor is that diagnosis replicable by independent observers. Instead, because mental illness is defined as a deviation from a set of "psychosocial and ethical" norms (Szasz 1963:14), the only way to diagnose the condition is to render a subjective judgment about the appropriateness of the "patient's" actions and attitudes. As an explanation of human behavior, the concept of mental illness is similar in several fundamental respects to the concepts of witchcraft or spirit possession. In each case, the condition is defined by consensus.

Ultimately, to say that a given person is an alcoholic is analogous to saying that the Mouton '59 is the century's finest wine. The first instance involves a diagnostic judgment while the second involves an aesthetic judgment, but in both cases the validity of the judgment can only be established by persuasive argument. In both cases, the key term in the assertion is vaguely defined, and the very ambiguity of the definition is what makes the assertion possible and plausible.

Obviously, the predilection for nonpropositional thinking is widespread, even among social scientists (or perhaps I should say especially among social scientists). Yet the danger of confusing emotive and propositional statements can be avoided if careful attention is paid to the nature of propositional claims. First and foremost, of course, any claim to propositional knowledge must be completely unambiguous—that is, it must state something clearly, precisely, and unequivocally. (The concept of mental illness fails to satisfy this necessary precondition for propositional status.) Beyond that, there are three criteria that any claim to propositional knowledge must satisfy in order to be considered warranted or valid.

First, of course, the assertion itself must be true. You hardly can claim to *know* that today is Friday if today in fact is Thursday. If people claim to *know* that the earth is flat, then they are making a statement of belief, not offering a claim to knowledge. Truth is a necessary condition for knowledge, although truth by itself is not knowledge, for reasons that I will discuss momentarily.

Second, you must *believe* that P is true (where P stands for any propositional statement—such as the claim that the sun sets in the west or the assertion that manatees are frequently confused with mermaids) in order to claim that you know P. If you *know* a proposition to be true, it would be absurd to say that you *believe* it to be false. You can believe something and not know it, but you cannot know something and not believe it. *Belief* is a necessary but not sufficient condition for knowledge.

Third, propositional knowledge must be substantiated by evidence— that is, you must have good reasons for believing *P* in order to claim that you know *P*. Wishful thinking or lucky guesses do not constitute knowledge. For example, you may believe that you hold the winning ticket in next week's lottery, and it might come to pass that in fact you do win the grand prize. The fact that you held a true belief, however, does not mean that you *knew* you would win. No knowledge is possible without some basis for knowledge. In addition, you cannot claim to have knowledge of any proposition if there is evidence that contradicts the truth of that proposition. Nor is the possession of reliable evidence sufficient to guarantee knowledge. We all have had the experience of being told the solution to a riddle and thinking that we should have been able to decipher it ourselves. *Evidence*, like truth and belief, is a necessary but insufficient condition for knowledge.

Collectively, however, these three criteria make up a sufficient condition for propositional knowledge. Any particular claim to knowledge is warranted if the claimant is making a true assertion about the world that he or she sincerely believes based upon sound evidence. No philosopher or reasonable person would deny that truth and belief are necessary conditions for propositional knowledge—but philosophers and reasonable people do disagree, and disagree frequently, about what constitutes sound evidence for knowledge. The pursuit of epistemology, therefore, most often is concerned with the question of evidence.

But what constitutes "sufficient evidence" for knowledge? What are the "good reasons" that substantiate and validate our claims to prop- ositional knowledge? These questions address the epistemological concern with the foundation of knowledge and challenge us to specify how we know what we know. They challenge us to examine our sources of knowledge.

The Source of Knowledge

There are several alleged bases for knowledge, some more reputable than others. Depending upon the manner in which they are concep- tualized, there are anywhere from at least four to more than a dozen different ways of knowing (Hospers 1967:122–141; Abel 1976:24–26; Chisholm 1977:122–123); here I will consider briefly seven purported epistemological foundations. Each of the following is used frequently to justify claims to knowledge:

1. *Sense Experience.* This is the most obvious and most common of all bases of knowledge. Knowledge obtained through sense experience is knowledge obtained by seeing, hearing, touching, tasting, and/or smelling. We have other physical senses, too, that are not always included within the traditional list of five basic senses, such as the kinesthetic sense that provides information about body motion and position. Yet sense experience is a problematic source of knowledge. Our eyes can perceive only a narrow range of the light spectrum; our ears only can register sounds ranging up to a limited number of cycles per second. Human beings are unable to sense magnetic fields or changes in barometric pressure (although, as biofeedback is teaching us, we are not sure what senses we may be able to develop). It is not just the *range* of our sensory perception that is limited, however. The possibility of hallucinations and mirages undermines our faith in the *accuracy* of sensory knowledge. More important than that, even, is the fact that sensory perception is an *indirect* path to knowledge. The human brain organizes sense data in particular ways dependent upon learning, context, experience, language, and a host of other variables. Environmental conditions, emotional and biochemical states, and learned preconceptions contribute to make sensory perceptions subjective and changeable. Any act of sensory perception is a selective act of interpretation.

This does not mean, of course, that we can never trust our senses; indeed, we have no choice but to trust the knowledge we acquire through sense experience. As the philosopher Reuben Abel (1976:30) explains, "The cure for the shortcomings of our senses is not to stop using them, but to use them critically and to be aware of these shortcomings. Errors in perception are corrected by more discriminating perception."

2. *Logic.* This foundation for knowledge is concerned only with the validity of inference and tells us whether a conclusion is justified by its premises. Thus we know that Socrates is mortal if we know that Socrates is a man and that all men are mortal, but our knowledge of Socrates' mortality is justified only if it is *true* that Socrates is a man and that all men are mortal—and logic alone cannot establish the truth of those premises. That is why Descartes elevated reason above experience; when he said, "I think, therefore I am," he depended upon no empirical premises. Reason alone, however, will not yield knowledge of the external world.

Logic, in other words, is a set of rules for determining the validity of any argument, and many of those rules have been formalized and named. *Modus ponens,* for example, is the name given to a valid form of argument that takes this pattern: If *P*, then *Q*; *P*; therefore *Q*. *Modus tollens* is the name applied to arguments that follow this particular form: If *P*, then *Q*; not *Q*; therefore not *P*. There are many other valid forms of argument that have been recognized and named, including hypothetical syllogisms, dilemmas, and contrapositions (see Cornman and Lehrer 1968:5–13). It is hardly necessary to memorize every valid form of argument, however. In order to determine the validity of any particular argument, it is sufficient to apply the method of counterexample—that is, can you find just one instance—even a hypothetical instance—in which the argument's premises would be true but the conclusion would be false? If you can find such an instance, then the argument is not valid. Such is the case, for example, with this argument: All anthropologists strive not to be ethnocentric; Diana strives not to be ethnocentric; therefore Diana is an anthropologist. Because Diana could just as well be a novelist or a nuclear engineer, the argument is invalid. Logic is a reliable source of knowledge only if it is used properly.

3. *Authority.* I know that the moon is approximately a quarter-million miles from the earth because I accept the authority of astronomers. A claim to knowledge by authority is a claim that the information provided by an expert can be trusted. Whether an appeal to authority constitutes a legitimate basis for knowledge depends upon the legitimacy of the epistemological foundations upon which the authority's knowledge is based. In other words, how did the expert acquire his or her knowledge? If a satisfactory answer cannot be provided, then the authority is not reliable, and the claim to knowledge is not warranted.

4. *Consensus Gentium.* The consensus of the people, or common knowledge, is often claimed to be a basis of knowledge: "I know it's true because everybody knows it's true." How do you *know* that it is a good idea to wait two hours after eating before going swimming? How do you *know* that lightning never strikes twice in the same place? (In fact it often does.) A great many people claim to know that hard work, thrift, and perseverance are guarantors of material success in contemporary U.S. society—or that women, on the whole, are more emotional, intuitive, and capricious than men. *Consensus gentium,* obviously, is an entirely unreliable foundation for knowledge, yet it is a foundation to which frequent appeal is made.

5. *Intuition.* This basis for knowledge is perhaps best defined as unanalyzed inference. We claim to know something by intuition when we are certain of our information but are unable to specify the exact source of our knowledge. By appealing to intuition, you really do not describe how you know what you know. You are saying, instead, that you cannot or will not identify the source of your knowledge and that you are content not to try to do so. That is not an intellectually defensible position, however. Different people have different intuitions about the same events, entities, and relationships, and thus there is no way to

distinguish between accurate and inaccurate intuitions on purely intu-
itional grounds.

6. *Revelation*. Many people claim to have acquired knowledge as the
result of communication (through dreams, visions, visitations, sacred
books, and the like) with the supernatural realm. But the revelatory
knowledge claimed by different people is often contradictory. (Some
people believe, by revelation, that Jesus Christ is the son of God; others
believe, also by revelation, that the true Messiah has yet to come.) How
is it possible to tell a true revelation from a false one? To everyone but
the claimant, revelation is indistinguishable from intuition.

7. *Faith*. Many people claim to know that God exists because they
have faith in God's existence. Those who appeal to faith as a basis for
knowledge claim, illogically, that the strength of their belief somehow
guarantees the certainty of their belief. If faith could establish knowledge,
then we could claim to know anything that we could imagine. The
epistemological foundation of faith is unsupportable. Belief alone is not
sufficient to establish propositional knowledge, for reasons that already
have been discussed. A person who claims to have knowledge by faith
does not have a good reason for claiming propositional knowledge.

There are other sources and supposed sources of knowledge. We
justify our claims to knowledge of our own emotional and cognitive
states by appeal to *self-awareness* (it would be pointless to ask people
how they know that they are angry). *Memory* affords a problematic
knowledge of past events. Some people claim to have direct *extrasensory*
knowledge of other people's thoughts. Most claims to knowledge—and
all those claims with which this book is concerned—are based upon
one or more of these seven sources of knowledge. All of them—sense
experience, logic, authority, *consensus gentium*, intuition, revelation, and
faith—are fallible. This does not absolve us of the obligation to justify
our claims to knowledge, however. Each of these seven ways of knowing
may be problematic, but they are not all equally valuable.

Epistemological Responsibility

No single source of knowledge is totally reliable at all times in all
situations, but it would be folly to conclude that reliable knowledge
thus is unobtainable. Because it is always possible that your senses may
deceive you, you cannot know with absolute certainty that you are
reading a book at this moment—but neither can you reasonably doubt
it. The position of unqualified and uncompromising epistemic skepticism—that is, that no claim to knowledge is *ever* warranted—is, as the
philosophers Cornman and Lehrer (1968:111) maintain, "a sham and a
delusion." We cannot lead human lives without acting as though we

do have knowledge about the world. Our claims to knowledge are pragmatically justified by the fact that our epistemic assumptions allow us to predict and control the world. Our claims to knowledge are more than simply expedient assumptions, however. The first criterion of propositional knowledge, remember, is that the proposition must be true. Yet there are those who claim that objective truth is either unattainable or nonexistent.

Phenomenology is the name of the philosophical school that holds that "reality" exists only as it is defined by human observers (Schutz 1967; Douglas 1970). Given that there are different human observers with different cultural backgrounds, different experiences, different attitudes, and different expectations, there are necessarily different realities—or so runs the phenomenological argument, at least in its simplest form. Perception, after all, requires interpretation, and the phenomenologists conclude that no one interpretation is any more real or true than another. Different witnesses to a crime or accident commonly report quite different details of the event; phenomenologists argue that no report, whether the victim's, the police officer's, or the bystander's, is anything other than one particular subjective account.

In many ways, the arguments of the phenomenologists are more subtle and more complex than my brief summation might suggest. Ultimately, however, all forms of phenomenology are guilty of the same logical error: They all transmute legitimate doubt into radical skepticism. The problem of objective reality is a genuine problem in philosophy, but it is not, as the phenomenologists argue, a necessarily insoluble problem.

To appreciate the error of the phenomenological viewpoint, consider the example of the traffic accident witnessed by several people from several different cognitive, emotional, and physical vantage points. Either there is or there is not a standard, objective version of the event—in other words, there either is or is not a version that is existentially valid independent of any observer. If there is such a version, why is it not possible that one of the observers could have produced an account that agreed with it, even if purely by coincidence? Why would it not be possible to develop epistemological procedures that consistently would apprehend the objective version of any event? Why is it a logical impossibility for any "constituted reality" to agree with objective reality? There is no reason. The barriers to objective knowledge are empirical, not logical. Moreover, the phenomenological argument is doomed either way. If there is *no* objective version of the accident, then what in the world happened to inspire the different interpretations?

We know the world exists; we know that events happen in the world. If we cannot claim to know these things, then there is little point in any discourse whatsoever about the nature and source of knowledge. The empirical barriers to knowledge challenge us to develop epistemological procedures that will yield consistently reliable knowledge. We cannot attain absolute certainty, but we can seek knowledge in a responsible fashion. Epistemological responsibility demands that we seek the greatest degree of certainty possible. In other words, epistemological responsibility demands that we continually evaluate how we know what we know.

There is a simple test to determine whether any epistemological foundation meets the standards of responsible inquiry: Is the knowledge obtained from that foundation self-correcting? In other words, is it possible to use the standards of a given epistemological foundation to distinguish a true claim to knowledge from a false one? This is perhaps best explained by example. If one person claims to know, by revelation, that Jesus Christ is the messiah, and another claims to know, also by revelation, that God has not yet sent a messiah, whose revelation is correct? Obviously both cannot be true; at least one must be false. But which? If the revelatory experiences seem to the two claimants to be equally strong, unequivocal, and compelling, how can we decide who has the true revelation? Do true revelations come only to sober people? Do they come only in well-lit rooms? Do they come only to true believers? The epistemological foundation of revelation contains no guidelines that will help us distinguish a true revelation from a false one.

Notice, however, that the foundation of sense experience is a different matter. If one person claims to know, by experience, that the earth is flat (a conclusion that would be eminently justified by most everyday sense experience), and another person, say an astronaut, claims to know by experience that the earth is round, we can appeal to sense experience to decide who is correct. Give the flat-earth advocate a view of the earth from an orbiting platform, and he or she will agree that the planet is indeed a sphere—provided that he or she is honest, sober, and possessed of normal eyesight.

The information obtained from sense experience may be misleading at times, but the validity of sense experience data can be checked and rechecked by independent observers in accordance with recognized standards and either confirmed or denied. If the same sensory observations are made by different people with different motives in different places at different times under different circumstances in response to the same stimulus and the results are the same, the knowledge obtained can be considered reliable with some degree of confidence. Logic yields infallible knowledge provided that the premises in question are true; it always is possible to recheck the steps used in logical analysis and to confirm or deny the validity of inference. Even authority is largely self-correcting because the authority's credentials can be rechecked and different authorities can be questioned (it always is possible to seek a second opinion, and there are standards for evaluating the claims of competing authorities—the unanimous judgment of fifty experts, for example, is to be trusted over the maverick opinion of a single expert), although, of course, the ultimate validity of knowledge obtained by authority rests upon the validity of the authority's epistemological foundations. Hence sense experience, logic, and authority are, to varying degrees and with certain obvious qualifications, responsible modes of inquiry.

Consensus gentium, intuition, revelation, and faith, however, are irresponsible epistemological foundations. None is self-correcting. *Consensus gentium* is unreliable; there are many different groups of people in the world with many different sets of commonly held beliefs, and the "knowledge of the people" therefore is variable and at times contradictory. Intuition, revelation, and faith are nothing more than rationalizations for the abrogation of epistemological responsibility. If different observers in different places at different times appeal to intuitive, revelatory, or emotive sources of knowledge, the results are very likely to be different and contradictory.

This is not to deny that intuition is frequently a valuable source of both inspiration and information. All of us use intuition all the time. We decide that our dinner companion is attracted to us on the basis of our intuitive knowledge of proxemics, body posture, pupillary reflex, and the like, and that decision is often well founded. At the same time, however, we have to recognize that intuition is fallible (sometimes embarrassingly so) and that correct intuitions are indistinguishable from incorrect ones. Both come to us with the same cachet of certainty. Granted, intuition is an indispensable source of artistic creativity and even scientific inspiration, but no claim to knowledge can ever be justified by an exclusive appeal to intuition. Revelation, faith, intuition, and *consensus gentium* cannot provide consistently reliable and trustworthy responses to the question "How do you know what you know?"

This brings us to science. The scientific approach is the only mode of inquiry that systematically and consistently appeals to self-correcting epistemological foundations. Marvin Harris (1979:6), one of the strongest advocates of the scientific approach in anthropology, maintains that "science is a superior way for human beings to obtain knowledge about the world in which we live." I would agree, with one important qualification (although it is a qualification that Harris recognizes): I would say that science is a superior way for human beings to obtain *propositional* knowledge about the world. Science probably will never give us the knowledge of how to write poetry, or how to translate languages, or how to create enduring works of art, but science will give us knowledge that will enable us to predict and control much of our world.

The epistemological value of science stems in large part from the fact that science is practiced by a critical community of scientists, and that fact has several important implications for the conduct of scientific inquiry and the advance of scientific knowledge. Before considering those implications, however, I will examine science and scientific explanation.

Suggestions for Further Reading

Reuben Abel's (1976) *Man Is the Measure* is an exceptionally well-written and engaging introduction to philosophical inquiry. For a somewhat more technical approach to the discipline of philosophy, John Hospers' (1967) *An Introduction to Philosophical Analysis* is one of the authoritative texts in the field. For an excellent collection of original works in the philosophy of science, see Klemke, Hollinger, and Kline (1980), *Introductory Readings in the Philosophy of Science.*

2

The Activity
of Science

The scientific approach is a relatively recent invention, but the impetus for scientific inquiry is as old as the human species. The philosopher Ernest Nagel (1961:4) attributes the motivation for science to the human need for reliable accounts of the world: "It is the desire for explanations which are at once systematic and controllable by factual evidence that generates science; and it is the organization and classification of knowledge on the basis of explanatory principles that is the distinctive goal of the sciences."

According to Nagel, the "systematic and controllable" nature of the scientific enterprise distinguishes science from "common sense." Commonsensical explanations, unlike scientific explanations, have limited applicability, are expressed in indeterminate language, and often are contradictory. The value of the scientific approach lies in its potential ability to overcome these shortcomings.

Scientific inquiry is predicated upon certain ontological assumptions (that is, assumptions about the nature of reality or existence), chief among them the assumption that an objective reality exists and is amenable to human inquiry. That assumption is shared by natural scientists and social scientists alike. The anthropologist Marvin Harris (1964:169), for example, writes that "the basic premise of empirical science is that there are things outside of the observer which no amount of merely logical manipulation can create or destroy." Science attempts to discover and explain the nature of those "things" in a precise, rigorous, and testable manner. The "distinctive aim of the scientific enterprise," according to Nagel (1961:15), "is to provide systematic and responsibly supported explanations."

However, the aim of the scientific enterprise is not to uncover "absolute truth." Science is a human enterprise, designed to serve human needs and interests. We apprehend and comprehend the universe in human terms. We can know only what we can perceive or infer; our instruments of perception are limited by our physiology and our ingenuity. Truth thus is best defined in pragmatic terms: A proposition is considered to be true if it enables us to make sense of the world. But the "truth" of any proposition always is subject to review. A proposition always can be replaced by another proposition that accounts for the world more reliably, more consistently, and more comprehensively. There is then no "final truth." Objective reality exists—if there was not something to be known, there would be no problem of knowledge—but objectivity is, in a sense, relative. It is relative to the needs, interests, goals, and sensory apparatus of human beings. As philosopher Michael Polanyi (1962) points out, objectivity requires a measure (relative to the amount of matter in the universe or to the age of the cosmos, the human species is an infinitesimal speck or an unnoticed flash). Reuben Abel (1976) makes clear that "Man" is the measure of objectivity. Science is intended to explain the "objective" nature of reality relative to human beings— and that is the only kind of objectivity that can truly concern us.

The anthropologists Pelto and Pelto (1978:22) suggest a definition of science that is provisionally acceptable: "Science is the structure and the processes of discovery and verification of systematic and reliable knowledge about any relatively enduring aspect of the universe, carried out by means of empirical observations, and the development of concepts and propositions for interrelating and explaining such observations."

That definition is adequate but for one omission—other than to say that the "processes of discovery and verification" are "carried out by empirical observations," Pelto and Pelto decline to specify exactly what those processes are. Scientific inquiry is conducted under the assumption that no concept, no fact, no idea is immune to critical scrutiny. Every scientific premise is a premise to be tested again and again and discarded if proven untrue. Thus Nagel (1961:13) says that "the practice of scientific method is the persistent critique of arguments." Abel (1976:81) maintains that "there is no single scientific method other than the unremitting criticism of evidence and reasoning in every way possible."

The Concept of Falsifiability

Scientific statements are critiqued in a special way. The philosopher Karl Popper (1959) has shown that scientific theories are never *verifiable;* what was proven true yesterday could logically be untrue tomorrow (the fact that the sun has risen every morning for the past 4 billion years does not mean that it will necessarily rise tomorrow). Rather than trying to verify theories, Popper (ibid.:41) argues that the scientific method consists instead of attempts to *falsify* them: *"It must be possible for an empirical scientific system to be refuted by experience"* (emphasis in original). If the real world of events and entities could never possibly disprove a given proposition, then there would be no limits, other than the limits of the human imagination, upon the content of that proposition. It must be possible to test a scientific assertion against the conditions of the world. Falsifiability, then, is the essential criterion of the scientific method. Popper (1963:256) maintains that "a system is to be considered as scientific only if it makes assertions which may clash with observations." By insisting that their claims to knowledge must be falsifiable, scientists simply are insisting that their theories must be propositional. The test of falsifiability is a convenient way of distinguishing between emotive and propositional statements.

If we accept the scientific criterion of falsifiability, we accept the responsibility to restrict our claims to knowledge to those assertions that could potentially be disproven. We must be able to specify what would make us abandon our beliefs. If we cannot do so, then our belief is vacuous; if anything and everything that could happen in the world would be congruent with our theory, then our theory says nothing. It is the same as if we had explained that things are the way they are because they are the way they are. If a claim to knowledge is not falsifiable, then it is not propositional. The challenge of science is the challenge to restrict ourselves to falsifiable beliefs.

However, some philosophers and scientists have objected that scientists rarely attempt to falsify their theories in practice, or if they do, they rarely accept evidence of falsification as sufficient grounds to discard a theory. Harris (1979:17–18), for example, argues that Popper neglects to specify at what point the evidence of falsification should be accepted as sufficient to falsify a theory. Popper's criterion of falsifiability, according to Harris (ibid.:17), fails to come to grips with scientific practice: "One black swan does not lead to the falsification of the belief that all swans are white but rather to such questions as: Is this black bird with a long neck really a swan?"

That point is well taken, but I think the thrust of Harris's criticism, and others like it, is wide of the mark. Popper (1959:86) recognizes that falsifiability and falsification are not the same thing; he maintains that any particular evidence of falsification must have a "reproducible effect" in order to falsify a theory (we would have to find an unexceptional number of black birds with long necks displaying swanlike characteristics before concluding that not all swans are white). Popper does not specify at what point contradictory evidence constitutes falsification because that specification is up to the individual scientist and is made with regard to a particular theory. Popper merely insists that scientific practice consists, or should consist, of the precise identification of the point of falsification. As Imre Lakatos (1970:92) argues, "Intellectual honesty consists . . . in specifying precisely the conditions under which one is willing to give up one's position."

I suggest, therefore, that science can be usefully defined in the following manner: Science is a systematic method of inquiry based upon empirical observation that seeks to provide coherent, reliable, and testable explanations of empirical phenomena and that rejects all accounts, descriptions, and analyses that are either not falsifiable or that have been decisively falsified. In short, science is an attempt to acquire knowledge that is objectively valid—although I use the word "objective" guardedly and with some trepidation. The term carries a particular meaning for scientists and should not be confused with dogmatic positivism, or the notion that perception is a direct path to knowledge (the charge most often made by critics of the scientific approach). According to Frank Cunningham (1973:4), scientific objectivity implies two things. First, objectivity means that accounts, descriptions, and analyses of a phenomenon should be offered without regard for the observer's thoughts and feelings about that phenomenon. Second, objectivity means that two rival theories about a given phenomenon cannot both be correct.

Objectivity, in other words, is essentially an epistemological construct; it is an agreement among scientists about the appropriate ways of gaining knowledge. The point to be stressed here is that individual scientists do not establish the objectivity of science. Objectivity is the result of the social nature of the scientific enterprise. This is an issue upon which virtually all philosophers of science agree. Carl Hempel (1965:334) maintains that scientific theories are objective if they are "capable of test by reference to publicly ascertainable evidence." Charles Frankel has offered the definitive defense of scientific objectivity.

> There are two principal reasons why scientific ideas are objective, and neither has anything to do with the personal merits or social status of individual scientists. The first is that these ideas are the result of a cooperative process in which the individual has to submit his results to the test of public observations which others can perform. The second is that

these ideas are the result of a process in which no ideas or assumptions are regarded as sacrosanct, and all inherited ideas are subject to the continuing correction of experience (1955:138–139).

"In the entire course of prehistory and history," writes Harris (1979:27), "only one way of knowing has encouraged its own practitioners to doubt their own premises and to systematically expose their own conclusions to the hostile scrutiny of nonbelievers." The scientific approach is our best strategy for overcoming the practical barriers to propositional knowledge about the empirical world.

Scientific Explanation

We use the word *explanation* in various ways to indicate the answers to questions of who, what, when, how, or why, but it is generally agreed that scientific explanations are concerned with the answers to *why* questions. It is difficult to pin down exactly what we mean by explanation. "Very broadly speaking," says Hempel (1965:425), "to explain something to a person is to make it plain and intelligible to him [or her]." The philosopher John Hospers (1968:78) notes that an explanation always is offered in terms of something other than the thing to be explained, although the criteria for explanatory adequacy are hard to define: "In any given case the explanation that will satisfy us depends on our intent in asking the question." In Abel's (1976:91) appropriate metaphor, "The explanation releases the tension that provoked the question." (Explanations by metaphor and analogy, incidentally, are often the most satisfying kind.)

As Hempel (1965:489) observes, "There is no sufficiently clear generally accepted understanding as to what counts as a scientific explanation." According to Hospers (1968:69–72), explanations of why something occurs or takes the form it does are offered in many different ways. Thus we explain by referring to the purpose of a phenomenon, by showing a particular event to be an instance of a familiar class of events, by classing an event as an instance of a general law, by identifying intermediate factors relating two phenomena, or by describing the "cause" of a phenomenon. Nagel (1961:21) maintains that scientists explain things in one of four ways: by deducing the explanation from a set of premises in which that explanation is logically entailed, by identifying probabilistic causes, by pointing out functional relationships, or by tracing historical connections. However, Hempel has offered what is probably the most comprehensive and most useful analysis of scientific explanation. According to Hempel (1965), all scientific explanations conform broadly to one of two types: deductive-nomological and statistical-probabilistic explanations.

In deductive-nomological explanations, the phenomenon to be explained is presented as the conclusion of a deductive argument. Deductive-nomological explanations show that the phenomenon in question could not have been avoided given the particular circumstances and the application of general laws (Hempel 1965:337). Thus we explain that the gas in the cylinder expanded when heated by reference to the general law that the density of gas in a volume is determined by the temperature of the gas. Not all deductive-nomological explanations are causal explanations, however. According to Hempel, many deductive-nomological explanations appeal to "laws of coexistence" (ibid.:352). Abel (1976:93), too, says that a "scientific explanation need not be a causal law," despite the common misconception that it should be. Hospers (1968:72), however, observes that "causality" is a vague and ambiguous term and declares that "so loosely is this weasel-word used that I feel safe in saying that every explanation is in *some* sense or other a causal explanation" (emphasis in original).

The invariable association of a band level of political organization with a hunting and gathering subsistence strategy is an example of a deductive-nomological law in anthropology. A subsistence strategy that requires small-group mobility cannot support a complex, centralized political structure because such structures require large, sedentary populations—hence we conclude, deductively, that foraging societies must display a level of political organization commensurate with their size (Carneiro 1967; Lee and DeVore 1968; 1977).

Statistical-probabilistic explanations come in two varieties: deductive and inductive. The first constitutes a fairly special case and is employed when a deductive conclusion is drawn from a set of statistical laws—as, for example, when we explain that the fiftieth toss of a coin has an equal probability of turning up heads or tails regardless of the outcome of the previous forty-nine tosses (Hempel 1965:380). The equal probability of heads or tails on the fiftieth toss is explained by reference to two statistical laws: one, that a random toss of a coin has a 50 percent probability of turning up heads, and two, that the probability associated with any single flip of the coin is independent of all previous tosses. Thus we conclude deductively that the fiftieth toss has a 50 percent probability of showing heads.

Inductive varieties of statistical-probabilistic explanations are much more common. Inductive statistical explanations show that the phenomenon in question was to have been expected, even though it may not have been logically necessary. Hempel (1965:381) offers as an example a patient who was cured of a streptococcus infection by the administration of penicillin. Not all patients suffering from streptococcus will be cured if given penicillin; some will die or develop other infections from other causes. But we explain the patient's recovery by reference to the inductive-statistical law that holds that streptococcus patients given penicillin very often are cured. That explanation releases the tension that provoked the question even though it described not what necessarily had to happen but only what was likely to happen.

The usual correspondence between a society's postmarital residence rules and its system of descent-reckoning is an example of a statistical-probabilistic law in anthropology. Most but not all matrilocal societies have matrilineal descent; the same correspondences can be found between patrilocality and patrilineality and between neolocality and bilaterality. These associations are not necessarily or inevitably true, but a sample of the world's societies shows them to be generally true and allows us to infer an inductive statistical law (Murdock 1949; Graburn 1971; Keesing 1975).

Deductive-nomological explanations may constitute the ideal of scientific explanation, but statistical-probabilistic explanations are commonly used, especially in the social sciences. As Hempel explains, statistical-probabilistic explanations are accepted to the extent that they consider the total evidence available. In what has been a controversial (but, I think, supportable) position, Hempel has maintained that both types of scientific explanation appeal to general covering laws. The "laws" invoked by a particular explanation may be implicit, but lurking behind every scientific explanation is some generalized principle. (Remember that Nagel says that scientific explanations have wide applicability.) It is important to keep in mind, however, that scientific explanations come in a variety of guises. There is no single criterion for scientific explanation other than empirical vulnerability.

Another way of saying that all scientific explanations appeal to general covering laws is to say that all scientific explanations are scientific theories. It is equally true to say, as Manners and Kaplan (1968:7) do, that all scientific theories are explanations. Theories answer *why*; they are "generalizations . . . which relate classes or types of phenomena to one another in certain determinate ways" (ibid.). Facts are explained once they have been subsumed under a set of theoretical statements, although the facts themselves are determined by the theory. In the strictest sense of the term, there is no such thing as an "objective" fact. Perception is selection and interpretation; theory tells the scientist what to select and how to interpret it. Good theory explains not just the special case (like catastrophism in geology), but all related cases. The function of theory is to decide whether any two cases are related. Ideally, good theory relates cases that previously were thought unrelated. Reuben

Abel (1976:83) says "a theory is arrived at . . . by a leap of the imagination to a new unifying idea." Scientific theories and explanations should be parsimonious—that is, they should account for much with little. But parsimony has a relative rather than an absolute value. If a theory explains everything it explains nothing. Every fact in the world, for example, is congruent with the explanation "Allah wills."

Scientific theories are not forged in isolation. They are produced in conjunction with other theories derived from a common set of theoretical principles and assumptions. Since the early 1960s, those sets of common principles—called "paradigms"—have been the focus of considerable attention in the philosophy of science. The next chapter explores the nature of scientific paradigms in detail.

Suggestions for Further Reading

The nature of science and scientific explanation are widely discussed in the philosophical literature, but some principal works in the philosophy of science are *The Logic of Scientific Discovery* and *Conjectures and Refutations*, by Karl Popper (1959; 1963); *The Structure of Science*, by Ernest Nagel (1961); and *Aspects of Scientific Explanation and Other Essays in the Philosophy of Science*, by Carl Hempel (1965). For a wide-ranging (although in my view ultimately mistaken) criticism of the scientific enterprise, see *Against Methods*, by Paul Feyerabend (1975).

3

The Concept
of Scientific Paradigms

The notion of scientific paradigms is most closely associated with the philosopher Thomas Kuhn. Kuhn (1970a) developed the concept of paradigmatic inquiry in an attempt to account for certain obvious anomalies in the history of science. Most contemporary philosophers of science agree that the idea of scientific development by accumulation is untenable. Scientific progress is not an exclusively incremental matter. Modern chemistry is built upon a rejection, not a refinement, of phlogistic chemistry. Einstein's theory of relativity has supplanted Newtonian physics, but it is difficult to argue that the scientists of Newton's day were less scientific in their approach or less rational than modern scientists. What then accounts for the difference? Why and how do sciences change and develop? It is to these questions that the concept of paradigmatic research is applied.

In *The Structure of Scientific Revolutions*, Kuhn (1970a:175) uses the term *paradigm* in two distinct senses: "On the one hand, it stands for the entire constellation of beliefs, values, techniques, and so on shared by the members of a given community. On the other, it denotes one sort of element in that constellation, the concrete puzzle-solutions which, employed as models or examples, can replace explicit rules as a basis for the solution of the remaining puzzles of normal science."

That second sense of *paradigm* is what Kuhn (1977:471) calls "exemplars"—the shining examples of successful research that members of a given scientific community hold as ideals. Scientific communities are composed of individuals who have essentially the same training, share the same goals, and refer to the same literature. Scientific communities are characterized by relatively full communication among their members and by relatively unanimous agreement on matters of professional judgment within their ranks (ibid.:461). Scientific communities, in short, are composed of scientists who share the same exemplars. Malinowski's Trobriand ethnography might be considered an anthropological exemplar.

That first sense of paradigm—paradigms as constellations of beliefs and techniques—has been most influential. Kuhn (ibid.:463) refers to a paradigm in this sense as a "disciplinary matrix"; others have used the terms *research program* (Lakatos 1970), *research tradition* (Laudan 1977), and *scientific research strategy* (Harris 1979). Disciplinary matrices define the problem for research and specify the appropriate methods of research. This is especially important to an understanding of how science works. Theory and fact are interpenetrating. The kinds of questions we ask determine the kinds of answers we get, and that is why the anthropologist Bob Scholte (1980:76–77) says that "the critical importance of a paradigmatic stance becomes especially evident in considering the question of 'fact.'"

In sum, then, paradigms consist of particular ontological assumptions and particular epistemological principles and embody as well a set of theoretical principles, from which, ideally, specific testable theories are derived. Perhaps most importantly, paradigms include a definition of the appropriate domain of inquiry to which those epistemological and theoretical principles are to be applied. As paradigms become established, they accumulate a body of particular explanatory theories. (Especially successful applications of theory, then, become exemplars.)

Particular scientific disciplines may include one or more paradigms (here and throughout the remainder of this book I use paradigm to mean disciplinary matrix or scientific research strategy). Paradigms are roughly synonymous with what were once referred to as disciplinary schools. Anthropology, as we shall see in Part 3, has several rival paradigms competing for the allegiance of contemporary researchers. Historical particularism and diffusionism are examples of anthropological paradigms that are no longer popular in the anthropological community. It is important to remember that paradigms themselves are not falsifiable because they are neither true nor false. The specific theories produced by scientific paradigms, however, are or should be falsifiable.

What then do paradigms have to do with the conduct and development of science? In the usual course of events, Kuhn argues, scientists are concerned with solving the puzzles presented by the paradigms under which they are working. Normal scientific activity consists of attempts to expand the knowledge of facts revealed (or, if you prefer, defined) by the paradigm. Most of the time, then, scientists have three broad paradigmatic concerns: first, to determine the facts at hand; second, to compare those facts with the paradigm's theoretical predictions; and third, to demonstrate and articulate the paradigm's theoretical principles (Kuhn 1970a:25–28). According to Kuhn (1970b:250), these activities constitute "normal science," which is "the generally cumulative process by which the accepted beliefs of a scientific community are fleshed out, articulated, and extended."

In the pursuit of normal science, scientists occasionally encounter new and unsuspected phenomena with which the existing paradigm cannot deal successfully (Kuhn 1970a:52). Initially, scientists respond to the awareness of anomaly by challenging the observations that identified the intractable fact and by adjusting the theories that attempt to explain it (Kuhn 1970b:13). If modifications to the paradigm are not sufficient to account for the perceived anomalies, however, normal science will give way to science in crisis, and the old paradigm will be overthrown and replaced by a new paradigm that has transformed the anomalous into the expected (Kuhn 1970a:77). These "scientific revolutions" are the "central episodes in scientific advance" (Kuhn 1970b:241).

Thus Kuhn argues that normal scientific activity does not consist simply of attempts to falsify theories. Tests are performed frequently in normal science, but they are tests of the scientist's ingenuity at puzzle solving, not tests of the theories themselves (Kuhn 1970b:5). Theories are not tested until the advent of a crisis. "Only when they must choose between competing theories do scientists behave like philosophers" (ibid.:7).

This may seem like a direct challenge to the appropriateness of Popper's falsifiability criterion, and, indeed, Popper has perceived it as such. Popper (1970:52) accepts Kuhn's contention that normal scientific activity is not concerned with the critical evaluation of fundamental theoretical assumptions but considers that state of affairs to be a serious threat to the scientific enterprise: "'Normal' science . . . exists. It is the activity of the non-revolutionary, or more precisely, the not-too-critical professional; of the science student who accepts the ruling dogma of the day; who does not wish to challenge it."

Kuhn, however, is not arguing for the abandonment of the falsifiability criterion as the essential standard of scientific legitimacy. He simply is observing that in practice scientists are not and could not be strict falsificationists. Uncompromising falsificationism would require that scientific theories be stated in such a way that any event could be classified as either a confirmation or a disconfirmation of the theory, unless it were irrelevant to the theory. As Kuhn (1970b:16) remarks, "No scientific theory satisfies those rigorous requirements." In normal science, no evidence of disconfirmation is absolutely conclusive; some adjustment or modification of the theory is always possible. Even Kuhn's critics agree with him on this point. Lakatos (1970:97), for example, maintains that "dogmatic falsificationism . . . is untenable."

Kuhn is not arguing that actual science and ideal science are irreconcilable. Falsifiability is the essential criterion of the scientific approach; it is the criterion by which any scientific explanation is to be evaluated. Kuhn simply argues that we cannot understand the growth and development of science if we look simply for evidence of falsificationism at work. Paradigms are not abandoned because their theories have been falsified; they are abandoned because they have been replaced by other paradigms that account for the anomalies for which the original paradigm could not account. The anthropological paradigm of structural-functionalism, for example, was not abandoned because its theories were disproved; it was abandoned because it was replaced by other paradigms (initially neoevolutionism and cultural ecology) that could account for sociocultural change—something structural-functionalism could not do and something anthropologists increasingly wanted to do.

But what factors precipitate the awareness of anomaly? At what point do scientists become dissatisfied with their paradigms? This is one of the thorniest problems facing Kuhnian analysis. Lakatos (1970:178) says that "there is no particular rational cause for the appearance of a Kuhnian 'crisis.'" Laudan (1977:74) criticizes Kuhn for the "arbitrariness" of the crisis point in normal science that gives rise to the scientific revolution. In response, Kuhn (1970a:65) argues that novelty emerges against a paradigmatic backdrop; the scientist committed to a particular paradigm knows with precision what to expect in terms of an "observation-theory match" and thus is able to recognize the occurrence of unanticipated facts. "Failure of existing rules is the prelude to a search for new ones" (Kuhn 1970a:68).

It is often difficult, however, for scientists to recognize that the existing rules have failed unless those rules have been compared with other rules that have been successful. Again, paradigms are not simply abandoned; they are replaced by other paradigms. Lakatos (1970:116) maintains that the history of science is the succession of "progressive problem shifts." In his view, the crisis that precipitates the revolution is the appearance of a progressive paradigm. Lakatos (ibid.:119) argues, in effect, that paradigms are progressive if they anticipate the unanticipated:

"A given fact is explained scientifically if a new fact is also explained with it."

That seems unobjectionable enough—more productive paradigms are better than less productive paradigms. Kuhn would agree, for he suggests that scientists regard "better" paradigms as those paradigms with greater "accuracy, scope, simplicity, fruitfulness, and the like" (1970b:261). But all of this leaves essentially unresolved the question of what engenders paradigmatic disenchantments among practicing scientists. Why and how are old paradigms rejected in favor of new ones? Kuhn (ibid.:19) admits "there is much about these questions that I do not understand and must not pretend to." In all probability, scientific revolutions are inspired partly by the failure of existing rules and partly by the attraction of promising new rules. New rules, of course, are created to account for the failure of old rules, but the failure of old rules is defined at least partially by the existence of new rules. Fact and theory are interpenetrating.

The most significant point of contention between Kuhn and his critics, however, does not involve the ticklish problem of paradigm shifts. Rather, it concerns the question of paradigmatic commensurability, or the question of whether rival paradigms can be compared and evaluated according to a standard measure. Paradigms incorporate a definition of the problems to be investigated and a specification of the techniques to be used in the solution of those problems. Kuhn argues that paradigms that define different problems for investigation and specify different means of solution are incommensurable. In the comparison and evaluation of incommensurable paradigms, the substantive contents of the paradigms cannot be compared simply and directly. Any two rival paradigms must share some standards of appropriateness in order for their proponents to agree upon questions of paradigmatic merit. In a debate between incommensurable paradigms, "the premises and values shared by the two parties . . . are not sufficiently extensive for that" (Kuhn 1970a:94). The participants in debates about incommensurable paradigms often talk past one another. "Each paradigm will be shown to satisfy more or less the criteria that it dictates for itself and to fall short of a few of those dictated by its opponent" (ibid.:110).

Not all paradigms are incommensurable. If two paradigms agree about the nature of the problem to be solved and about the appropriate means of solving that problem, they are commensurable. Furthermore, paradigmatic commensurability is a relative matter. Two paradigms may agree about the problem to be investigated but disagree as to the means of solution. Scientific evolution and "scientific creationism," for example, are both concerned with the origins of the human species, but the two paradigms have radically different epistemological principles. If one paradigm chooses to rely upon experience as its epistemological foundation, it can make no impact upon a paradigm that appeals ultimately to revelation. If the participants in such a debate restrict themselves to the terms and assumptions of their own paradigms, they can have nothing to say to one another. (This is why epistemology is the common ground in all debates, whether the debate involves commensurable or incommensurable theoretical positions. Eventually, all unresolved substantive issues boil down to a disagreement about epistemology.)

Critics have railed against the concept of paradigmatic incommensurability. Popper (1970:56) says that "it is just a dogma—a dangerous dogma—that the different frameworks [of rival paradigms] are like mutually unintelligible languages." Lakatos (1970:178) interprets paradigmatic incommensurability to mean that "there are no rational standards for their comparison [because] each paradigm contains its own standards." He faults Kuhn for arguing, purportedly, that there is no way to judge a theory except by "assessing the number, faith, and energy of its supporters" (ibid.:93). Harris (1979:21) accuses Kuhn of failing to believe in "the inherent progressivism of scientific knowledge."

What disturbs these critics most is the notion that the incommensurability of paradigms would preclude the evaluation of paradigms. Laudan (1977:71) insists that the evaluation of paradigms is a comparative matter: "What is crucial in any cognitive assessment of a theory is how it fares with respect to its competitors." Popper (1970:57) comes to the same conclusion: "Thus in science, as distinct from theology, a critical comparison of the competing theories, of the competing frameworks, is always possible. And the denial of this possibility is a mistake."

Each of these critics has misread Kuhn. Yes, the evaluation of paradigms is a comparative matter. Yes, it would be a mistake to deny the necessity of theoretical comparison. But Kuhn does not deny that necessity, nor does he deny the fact of scientific progress. Kuhn (1970a:206) states unequivocally that he is "a convinced believer in scientific progress." What Kuhn does deny is the possibility that the comparison and evaluation of two incommensurable paradigms can be made in the terms of one paradigm or the other. To fault a paradigm for its failure to grant its competitor's theoretical principles or for its lack of interest in its competitor's research problems is to beg the question. To say that two rival paradigms are incommensurable is not to imply that the paradigms are of equal value, significance, productivity, or scientific merit. Granted, paradigms must be compared, but paradigmatic theories that address completely different questions are not themselves directly comparable.

Given that there is such a thing as scientific progress, it follows that some paradigms must be more progressive than others and thus that it must be possible to determine which paradigms are more progressive and why. Kuhn (1970a:296) suggests that superior paradigms are characterized by higher accuracy of prediction, greater precision of problem definition, and greater success at problem solution. It is a fairly straightforward matter to determine which of two commensurable paradigms is superior: simply ascertain which solves the stated problem more precisely, reliably, and accurately. But what about incommensurable paradigms? How are they to be evaluated?

The answer is twofold. In the first place, a paradigm must be evaluated in its own right, without reference to other incommensurable paradigms, according to the appropriateness of its internal logic. Does the paradigm fulfill its promise? Does it address meaningful questions consistently, coherently, and cogently? Is its field of inquiry sufficiently broad and sufficiently well defined? Does the paradigm produce theories that are testable and falsifiable? Are its solutions comprehensive and compelling? Does it leave significant problems within its domain of inquiry unsolved? These are the standards for the initial evaluation of incommensurable paradigms.

Second, incommensurable paradigms must be compared with reference to the question of value. Given two paradigms that address totally different questions, the debate must touch inevitably upon the issue of which paradigm addresses the most significant or important questions (Kuhn 1970a:110). Whether implicit or explicit, value positions are inseparable from the assumptions that underlie all paradigms. The question of value is an unavoidable question in the selection of scientific paradigms, but it is not a question that can be answered by science. Value is instead a moral and philosophical question and must be addressed on those grounds. These principles of paradigmatic comparison and evaluation will be illustrated in Part 3, when I review anthropological paradigms in some detail.

In summary, I have reached several conclusions in Part 1 of this book: first, that responsible inquiry entails critical appeal to the epistemological foundations of experience, logic, and authority; second, that the scientific approach is a preeminently valuable way of gaining knowledge about the empirical world; and third, that scientific research involves the construction and articulation of scientific paradigms. The scientific approach can be applied to a very wide range of questions. The problem with which I will be concerned in the chapters that follow is the nature of the human condition; the application of the scientific method to that problem is the subject of Part 2.

Suggestions for Further Reading

Thomas Kuhn's (1970a) *The Structure of Scientific Revolutions* is the seminal work on paradigmatic commensurability; for an alternative point of view, see *Progress and Its Problems*, by Larry Laudan (1977). *Criticism and the Growth of Knowledge*, by Lakatos and Musgrave (1970), is a collection of essays that provides a fair sample of the range of opinion on paradigmatic issues.

PART TWO

THE ANTHROPOLOGICAL PERSPECTIVE

My excuse for venturing across disciplines, continents, and centuries is that the world extends across disciplines, continents, and centuries.
—Marvin Harris,
Cows, Pigs, Wars and Witches

4

The Science
of Anthropology

Most historical accounts of the development of anthropology stress the fact that the discipline is hardly more than a century old. Anthropologists do trace the origins of their discipline back to the ancient Greeks, particularly to Herodotus (whose parentage anthropologists share with historians), but anthropologists only have been calling themselves anthropologists since the latter part of the nineteenth century. Although it is true that the origins of anthropology as a distinct discipline may be traced to such nineteenth century figures as Herbert Spencer, James Frazer, Edward B. Tylor, and Lewis Henry Morgan, anthropological inquiry is not new. Or, more appropriately, there is nothing new about the field of anthropological inquiry. In *Images of Man*, Annemarie de Waal Malefijt (1974:vii) correctly ascribes the origins of anthropological investigation to the "universal concern to understand human experience and human behavior." People have been asking questions about the relationships among human beings, nature, and culture for as long as there have been people. The contemporary discipline of anthropology is hardly original for having posed those same questions. The originality and merit of the discipline lie in the set of investigative approaches and theoretical assumptions that constitute the anthropological perspective. There is something new about the *method* of anthropological inquiry.

Everyone in the world holds theories about human nature, the meaning of human life, and human destiny; everyone is committed to some particular understanding of human personality and human society; and everyone accounts in some way for the facts of historical and cultural differences among the societies of the world. Most of the people in the world, of course, hold their theories implicitly, are uncritical of the epistemological foundations of their theoretical perspectives, and assume that their theories are isomorphic with the reality of the world. Further, no one in the world holds wholly original theories about the human condition. Explanations of, about, and for the human experience are central features of the cultural legacy of every society in the world. As a result, most people base what they know about human nature and human life primarily upon the epistemological foundations of *consensus gentium*, intuition, and authority.

Anthropology as Science

Anthropological knowledge, however, is distinct not only from folk knowledge, but also from psychological, sociological, theological, astrological, and other more or less systematic sources of knowledge, scientific and otherwise, about the human condition. This chapter and the chapters that follow in Part 2 explore the essential, distinguishing features of the anthropological perspective.

The first thing to be noted about that perspective is that it is, or could be, or perhaps should be a scientific perspective. The qualifications are necessary because there is hardly complete agreement among anthropologists as to whether anthropology is or is not a science. (There is further disagreement about whether anthropology is or should be "simply and narrowly" a social science.) Some contemporary anthropologists believe that the anthropological perspective derives its distinctiveness from the comprehensiveness of its approach. They hold that anthropology embraces the physical sciences, the social sciences, and the humanities simultaneously. According to that argument, anthropology's difference lies in the fact that anthropologists bring a unified, integrative viewpoint to bear on the human condition. Thus aesthetic analyses of folklore and statistical analyses of blood types are both appropriate activities for anthropologists to undertake, and the designation *science* is considered too narrow to encompass both endeavors. Given that literary analyses and the like are usually not scientific enterprises, the point at issue is whether anthropologists who wish to pursue such activities should properly claim to be "doing" anthropology. Or, if these anthropologists claim to be practicing anthropology, the question is whether anthropology should then claim to be a science.

In this book, I intend to follow well-established precedents and regard anthropology as a science. (My primary concern, of course, is with the social science of sociocultural anthropology.) If some anthropologists wish to pursue research under nonscientific paradigms, then I would have no objection and would not be jealous of the label *anthropology*, provided that the research questions to be investigated from a nonscientific perspective could not be better investigated from a scientific viewpoint. (The aesthetic analysis of art would be an example of the kind of research that would be better pursued via a nonscientific approach.) I maintain, however, that the central concern of sociocultural anthropology is to understand and explain human social life and human behavior, and I believe that goal can best be attained through scientific inquiry.

Scientific anthropology traditionally, and misleadingly, has been associated with ecological or materialist anthropology, primarily because ecological anthropologists have made the most consistent and explicit claims to a scientific approach. Julian Steward (1955:3), for example, regards his concept of multilinear evolution as an explicitly scientific approach, defining the "scientific approach" as an attempt "to arrange phenomena in orderly categories, to recognize consistent relationships between them, to establish laws of regularities, and to make formulations which have predictive value." However, he also contrasts the "scientific, generalizing approach" with the "historical, particularizing approach" and sows confusion by seeming to imply that science is not concerned with explaining either historical or particular, nonrecurrent events and entities. In *Theory of Culture Change*, Steward argues in effect that a scientific approach to anthropological inquiry necessarily would result in ecological anthropology. The confusion about science and history is absent from Harris's (1979:26) version of the scientific perspective; he contends that "the aim of scientific research strategies . . . is to account for observable entities and events and their relationships by means of powerful, interrelated parsimonious theories subject to correction and improvement through empirical testing." However, Harris also seems to equate the scientific perspective in anthropology with a particular paradigm addressed to a particular set of questions, rather than with a particular method of inquiry. Harris's *Cultural Materialism* is subtitled *The Struggle for a Science of Culture*, and his theoretical perspective is a direct descendant of Steward's (Harris 1968). Despite the traditional associations the term *science* has among anthropologists, the scientific approach is not confined exclusively to ecological anthropology.

Instead, the methodology of anthropological inquiry, addressed to whatever particular question, makes anthropology scientific. As Pelto and Pelto (1978:24) conclude, "Anthropology can be considered a science because it involves the accumulation of systematic and reliable knowledge about an aspect of the universe carried out by empirical observation and interpreted in terms of the interrelating of concepts referable to empirical observation." That assessment is widely shared among contemporary anthropologists, and most recent writers concerned with anthropological theory have chosen to regard anthropology as a science. Furthermore, most anthropologists accept Popper's notion that falsifiability is the essential criterion of the scientific approach. Thus Cohen (1970:32) says that "whether or not the theory is scientific depends ultimately on whether the ideas involved can be submitted to a test of their validity," and Naroll (1970:29) maintains that "scientific research . . . consists of the construction of general and elegant theories together with the systematic attempt to *dis*prove them." By these criteria, anthropology is a science.

In the past twenty-five years, archeologists have been more concerned with the scientific status of anthropology than have sociocultural anthropologists. The "new archeology," which appeared in the early 1960s, is an explicit and thoroughgoing attempt to make archeology scientific (Watson, LeBlanc, and Redman 1971; Redman 1973; Willey and Sabloff 1974). Archeologists tend to be more familiar with contemporary issues in the philosophy of science than are sociocultural anthropologists (see, for example, Salmon 1982; Renfrew, Rowlands, and Segraves 1982; Binford and Sabloff 1982), and archeologists are more likely than ethnologists to adopt strong positivist positions—Watson, LeBlanc, and Redman (1974:126), for example, endorse without qualification Hempel's contention that all scientific explanation is of the "covering law" type. Fortunately, most contemporary archeologists consider themselves to be first and foremost anthropologists; if they have shored the scientific foundations of archeology, then they have helped make anthropology as a whole more scientific.

By calling anthropology a science, I do not mean to imply that the discipline is culture free or that its practitioners are immune to cultural influences. Anthropology in particular and science in general are both products of a particular cultural tradition, and their development should be understood in that context. But to argue, as some anthropologists and philosophers do, that all science is simply ethnoscience—and that Western science is no better or worse than the folk tradition of any other culture—is to misunderstand science. The origins of the scientific perspective have nothing necessarily to do with the validity of the scientific approach, and to suggest otherwise is to commit a logical fallacy. Whether or not the scientific approach is uniquely valuable is an epistemological question, not a cultural or an historical one.

The Idea of a Social Science

Before moving on to a consideration of the particulars of the anthro-pological approach, I should take note of those who have challenged the very idea of a social science (see Hollis and Lukes 1982). It is often claimed that the social, or "soft," sciences are less scientific than the physical, or "hard," sciences because the social sciences cannot devise experiments in which all the variables are controlled and because the social sciences are unable to predict social events with absolute accuracy. Those criticisms stem from a misunderstanding of what science is and is not. Science is not a body of knowledge, or a particular set of research methodologies, or a laboratory exercise in the manipulation of impersonal quantitative data. Science is a way of gaining knowledge. Astronomers are for the most part unable to experiment with their data, and atomic physicists routinely make probabilistic predictions that fall far short of absolute accuracy. Empirical vulnerability is the essential criterion of science, and that criterion applies whether scientific inquiry is conducted in the laboratory or elsewhere.

A more significant challenge to the appropriateness of social science is associated with the term *Verstehen* (to understand). Those philosophers of science who subscribe to the *Verstehen* position insist that the methods of the physical sciences cannot be applied to the social sciences because human beings, unlike inanimate matter or energy, inhabit artificial worlds of meaning. In order to understand human action, runs the argument, the social scientist must empathize with the subjects of his or her research. Peter Winch (1958) argues that social scientific investigation is different in kind from physical scientific investigation because the object of the social scientist's research responds to the presence of the social scientist. Thus simply by studying his or her data the social scientist unavoidably alters them.

It is true that social scientists are very likely to alter the data they are studying and that people imbue their activities with meaning, thereby challenging the social scientist to take account of the meanings in their heads, but these are practical problems, not logical ones. The requirements for scientific validity remain the same, regardless of the particular method or object of study. Obviously subatomic particles and human beings cannot be studied in the same way, but claims to knowledge about subatomic particles and human beings can be evaluated according to the same standards. For scientists, those standards include precision, reliability, objectivity, and falsifiability. Charles Frankel has succinctly and definitively dismissed the *Verstehen* argument.

Sympathetic identification . . . is neither sufficient nor essential to guarantee the discovery of truth in the human studies. It is not sufficient because the mistakes that people make when they think they have identified with others are notorious; it is not essential because it is possible to explain another person's behavior without identifying with him [of her]. It would be something of a nuisance if we tried to be schizophrenic while we studied schizophrenia. I conclude, therefore, that it is false to say that we understand the actions of other human beings "only because they are known to us from the working of our own minds" (1960:99).

Frankel's argument is, in my opinion, persuasive and unassailable, but there are many philosophers and scientists who remain unconvinced. Among anthropologists, there are two broad camps: those who believe that an objective social science is possible and those who believe that all social scientific investigation is necessarily subjective. Those who embrace the idea of an objective social science are known as rationalists or positivists; those who are sympathetic to the *Verstehen* position and the arguments of the phenomenologists are known as relativists. Bob Scholte summarizes the differences between the two.

The rationalist believes that universal standards of reason exist and that they may be context-free and thus irreducibly true. Therefore, translation, interpretation, and explanation are in fact possible and in principle true. The relativist, in contrast, believes that all standards of reason are in the final analysis local and conventional and thus context-dependent and reducible to identifiable sociocultural circumstances. Therefore, translation, interpretation, and explanation are in fact partial and in principle problematic (1984a:962).

Scholte is sympathetic to the relativist position, but I agree with the philosopher Charles Sanders Peirce: I cannot pretend to doubt in philosophical discourse what I do not doubt in my heart. Human existence is not a dream or an illusion. There is a reality to our lives, a reality that is independent of our individual or cultural perspectives. If that were not the case, it would be pointless to even talk about our knowledge of the human condition (who, or what, after all, would do the talking?). Because translation, interpretation, and explanation are problematic in principle does not mean that they are impossible in principle. To argue that the many impediments to knowledge about the social world make such knowledge logically unattainable is to despair in the face of a practical problem (it is also, as discussed earlier, to draw a conclusion that does not follow from the premises). The first response is emotionally unattractive; the second is intellectually indefensible. There is no compelling reason not to apply the scientific approach to human behavior. The question is not whether a science of anthropology is possible but whether it is practical. The answer is yes—a qualified yes, admittedly, but an unambiguous affirmative nonetheless.

Suggestions for Further Reading

For a good basic introduction to the science of anthropology, see *Culture Theory*, by David Kaplan and Robert Manners (1972). Pertti and Gretel Pelto (1978) offer a more sophisticated treatment of the topic in *Anthropological Research*. For an exhaustive collection of readings dealing with all aspects of anthropological science, see *A Handbook of Method in Cultural Anthropology*, by Naroll and Cohen (1970). See also Jarvie (1964; 1984), Bohannan and Glazer (1973), Naroll and Naroll (1973), Bee (1974), Malefijt (1974), Thoresen (1975), Voget (1975), Garbarino (1977), Harris (1968; 1979), Silverman (1981), Barrett (1984), and Ulin (1984).

5

The Domain
of Anthropological Inquiry

I have said that the anthropological perspective embodies theories about the relationships among human nature, human personality, human society, and human culture. Now I want to attempt a more precise definition of the domain of anthropological inquiry. The social philosopher Hannah Arendt (1958:2) makes the point that the human species is neither sui generis nor entirely unoriginal among the forms of life found on earth: "The human artifice of the world separates human existence from all mere animal environment, but life itself is outside this artificial world, and through life man remains related to all other living organisms."

Arendt's point is one that has been fundamental to the anthropological perspective since the inception of the discipline. The "human artifice" of culture is the primary adaptive mechanism of the human species. Throughout his career, Leslie White (1949; 1959) insisted upon a definition of culture as an extrasomatic, energy-capturing mechanism dependent for its existence upon the use of symbols. Clifford Geertz (1973:140) has been influential in the development of a contemporary paradigm addressed to the consequences and implications of the fact that "man is a symbolizing, conceptualizing, meaning-seeking animal." Loren Eiseley (1946:92), our discipline's most lyrical and poignant writer, characterizes "man" in this way: "Creature of dream, he has created an invisible world of ideas, beliefs, habits, and customs which buttress him about and replace for him the precise instincts of lower creatures."

To be human, then, is to live in a world that is both "real" and "artificial," or in a world that is both shared and not shared with other animal species. In other words, the human species faces two related but distinct tasks: the maintenance of human life and the maintenance of human identity.

By the maintenance of human life I mean those activities whose primary function is to satisfy the physical and metabolical requirements of survival. The maintenance of human life includes those activities that may be subsumed under the headings of subsistence, reproduction, health, and so on. The maintenance of human life invariably implies such considerations as the division of labor and the maintenance of social order because human physical needs are universally satisfied by cultural means.

By the maintenance of human identity I mean those activities whose primary function is to define and demarcate human status, or those activities whose express origin lies in the human tendency to impose symbol-mediated meanings upon the world. The maintenance of human identity involves such activities as art, music, and ritual, and it encompasses such issues as the formation of personality and the formulation of world view. *The Rites of Passage,* Arnold van Gennep's (1960; originally 1909) enduring classic of holocultural research, explores some of the processes by which human identity is maintained. The philosopher and social historian Johan Huizinga (1950:46) is concerned with the maintenance of human identity when he argues that play is the foundation of human culture: "Social life is endued with supra-biological forms, in the shape of play, which enhances its value. It is through this playing that society expresses its interpretation of life and the world."

The maintenance of human identity, in fact, is a problem often investigated by philosophers, artists, novelists, and other humanists, reinforcing the prejudice shared by many anthropologists that only the maintenance of human life can or should be investigated from a scientific perspective. The ways in which problems associated with the maintenance of human identity might be investigated from a scientific perspective will be discussed in Part 3.

A moment's reflection will reveal that a rigid distinction between the pursuit of life and the pursuit of identity cannot be maintained with respect to human activities. All, or at any rate a very substantial majority of all, human activities simultaneously involve the maintenance of human life and the maintenance of human identity. Religious activities are among the most significant ways in which human beings define themselves as human beings, yet the content and organization of religious beliefs and behaviors are closely linked to the particular cultural strategy of adaptation—a strategy whose most immediate and apparent function is the maintenance of human life. The phenomenon of voodoo death scarcely can be classed solely as a consequence of either the maintenance of human life or the maintenance of human identity; anthropological accounts of voodoo death have explained the phenomenon in terms of an interaction between the physiological and the psychological (Cannon 1942; Lex 1974). The human animal, apparently, is the only animal that can be killed by suggestion. The very essence of the human condition, in fact, is the intertwining of the maintenance of human life and the maintenance of human identity.

Nevertheless, I think it is useful to posit a distinction between these two dimensions of the human experience, for two reasons. First, it is a convenient way of distinguishing between the anthropological and the ethological domains of inquiry. (Despite Konrad Lorenz, we cannot study people in the same way that we study geese, nor does the study of one tell us very much about the other.) Second, it is useful because most contemporary anthropologists tend, in practice, to distinguish between the two when offering anthropological explanations and analyses. All anthropologists share the perspective that human life and identity are mutually interpenetrating, but, when defining their problems for research, most contemporary anthropologists choose to focus upon a problem that emphasizes one aspect or the other. I say "emphasizes" because no study of the human condition, obviously, can ignore entirely either aspect unless it defines its subject so narrowly that it is no longer studying any recognizable part of the human experience (sociobiology would be an example of such a reduction). Anthropologists have so far failed to develop a single paradigm that addresses both problems in a fully integrative fashion, as we shall see in Part 3.

I think I can demonstrate the usefulness of the distinction between the maintenance of human life and the maintenance of human identity by reference to a pair of contrasting examples. Roy Rappaport's (1967) classic article, "Ritual Regulation of Environmental Relations Among a New Guinea People," is an excellent illustration of the anthropological approach that focuses on the problems, consequences, and implications associated with the maintenance of human life. Rappaport's article is intended to counter the once common notion that ritual activity has no practical effect upon the external world other than such sociological and psychological functions as the preservation of social cohesion and the amelioration (or intensification) of anxiety. Rappaport demonstrates that Tsembaga ritual cycles play a significant role in the adjustment of the Tsembaga to their natural environment. Specifically, he shows that ritual activity regulates the distribution of land, the frequency of intergroup fighting, and the distribution of animal protein in the form of surplus pigs. In short, he examines and analyzes the ritual activities of the Tsembaga "as neither more nor less than part of the behavioral repertoire employed by an aggregate of organisms in adjusting to its environment" (Rappaport 1967:18).

Rappaport is well aware of the fact that he ignores the entire set of issues pertaining to the maintenance of human identity (even though he does not use that term), and he does so deliberately and without apology.

> Space does not permit a description of [the] ideological correlates [of the Tsembaga ritual cycle]. It must suffice to note that Tsembaga do not necessarily perceive all of the empirical effects which the anthropologist sees to flow from their ritual behavior. Such empirical consequences as they may perceive, moreover, are not central to their rationalizations of the performances. The Tsembaga say that they perform the rituals in order to rearrange their relationships with the supernatural world. We may only reiterate here that behavior undertaken in reference to their "cognized environment"—an environment which includes as very important elements the spirits of ancestors—seems appropriate in their "operational environment," the material environment specified by the anthropologist through operations of observation, including measurement (Rappaport 1967:22).

Rappaport is correct, of course, in his observation that Tsembaga ritual is no less than part of the adaptive behavior of a group of individuals. In addition, he is heuristically justified in regarding Tsembaga ritual as no more than such behavior because he thereby is able to demonstrate the practical consequences of supposedly "impractical" behavior. However, his decision to regard Tsembaga ritual as no more than adaptive behavior is merely a matter of convenience. Ritual is always "more" than adaptive behavior in part because no other species includes ritual activity in association with cosmological beliefs as part of its strategy for adaptation to its environment. The cosmological beliefs of the Tsembaga are irrelevant to the practical effects of Tsembaga ritual, but not irrelevant to what it means to be a Tsembaga. By focusing upon the maintenance of human life, it is possible to show why particular rituals and cosmologies take the form they do, but it is not possible to show why rituals and cosmologies exist in the first place. To explain the origin (rather than the maintenance) of ritual behavior, it is necessary to focus upon the maintenance of human identity.

"Deep Play: Notes on the Balinese Cockfight," a classic article by Clifford Geertz (1973:412–453), is an excellent sample of a study that deals exclusively with the maintenance of human identity. In the article,

Geertz takes pains to describe the elaborate Balinese cockfight in great detail. For the Balinese, as he explains, the cockfight is much more than a sport or entertainment; it is a complex symbolic event by means of which the Balinese define themselves. In Bali, a fighting cock is a highly charged symbol; it is, on one level, an expression of its owner's sexuality, but at the same time it represents danger, a direct moral and metaphysical inversion of human status. To participate in a cockfight, either as an owner, a handler, or a betting spectator, is to put oneself at risk. To participate in a cockfight, Geertz (ibid.:434) tells us, is to gamble not only one's money, but "one's pride, one's poise, one's dispassion, [and] one's masculinity" as well. In the end, the cockfight "is fundamentally a dramatization of status concerns" (ibid.:437). The cockfight is "a means of expression; its function is neither to assuage social passions nor to heighten them . . . but, in a medium of feathers, blood, crowds, and money, to display them" (ibid.:444).

In short, Geertz explores the meaning the cockfight holds for the Balinese. His concern is not with how the Balinese ensure their survival, but with how they perceive themselves and express themselves in a social world built upon shared, public meanings conveyed through symbols. His fundamental assumption is that "the imposition of meaning on life is the major end and primary condition of human existence" (ibid.:434), and his fundamental argument is that the Balinese accomplish that goal partly through the symbolic medium of the cockfight. In pursuing that kind of analysis, Geertz openly admits that he is looking at Balinese life from a peculiar perspective for a particular purpose.

> To put the matter this way is to engage in a bit of metaphorical refocusing of one's own, for it shifts the analysis of cultural forms from an endeavor in general parallel to dissecting an organism, diagnosing a symptom, deciphering a code, or ordering a system—the dominant analogies in contemporary anthropology—to one in general parallel with penetrating a literary text. If one takes the cockfight, or any other collectively sustained symbolic structure, as a means of "saying something of something" . . . then one is faced with a problem not in social mechanics but social semantics (ibid.:448).

The point of these illustrations is this: Like Rappaport and Geertz, most anthropologists narrow their fields of inquiry and analysis when addressing particular topics. Except when attempting comprehensive ethnographies, most anthropologists confine themselves to problems associated with either the maintenance of human life or the maintenance of human identity; a good many ethnographies have been written exclusively from one of those two viewpoints. In the conduct of scientific research, scientists inevitably focus upon those aspects of a given phenomenon that they consider most salient or noteworthy (or, at times, those aspects they believe to have been previously ignored), which is a decision based partly on personal interests and partly on paradigmatic commitment.

Whether anthropologists choose to focus upon questions associated with the maintenance of human life or the maintenance of human identity, they ideally should be aware that no anthropological explanation of any human activity is complete until the implications of both problems have been considered. The essence of the anthropological perspective, again, is the recognition that both factors are at play. The proper domain of anthropological inquiry consists of the origins, consequences, and implications of human efforts to maintain life and identity.

It is important to keep in mind at this stage, however, that the distinction between the maintenance of human life and the maintenance of human identity does not parallel the distinctions between behavior and thought, etics and emics, or materialism and idealism. The maintenance of human life and the maintenance of human identity include behavior *and* thought; both can be investigated from either an etic or an emic perspective; and the distinction between the two has nothing to do with arguments about the nature of cultural causality. Rather, the distinction is intended to highlight the essential characteristic of the human condition, which is that human beings are separated from all other forms of animal life by the "human artifice," while at the same time remaining related to all other forms of life by the fact of life itself. The "human artifice," in anthropological terms, is culture, and the concept of culture is the basic ingredient of the anthropological perspective. As such, the concept merits close scrutiny, and that is the task of the next chapter.

Suggestions for Further Reading

Among the best and most readable anthropological works dealing with issues associated with the maintenance of human life are Marvin Harris's popular books, especially *Cows, Pigs, Wars and Witches* (1974) and *Cannibals and Kings* (1977). For the quintessential anthropological approach to issues associated with the maintenance of human identity, see Clifford Geertz's (1973) *The Interpretation of Cultures.* Many of the articles I have published about my research in the British Virgin Islands deal specifically with the maintenance of human identity, especially "Ludic and Liminoid Aspects of Charter Yacht Tourism in the Caribbean" (Lett 1983) and "Playground in the Sun" (Lett 1985a); another paper, "The British Virgin Islands Tourism Industry" (Lett 1982), deals primarily with the maintenance of human life. The bibliographies of most anthropologists can be categorized similarly.

6

The Concept of Culture

"Know what [an anthropologist] thinks a savage is," writes Clifford Geertz (1973:346), "and you have the key to his [or her] work." If you know how an anthropologist defines culture, you will have a good idea of what he or she intends to study. The anthropological domain of inquiry encompasses the maintenance of human life and the maintenance of human identity, and the fundamental premise of the anthropological perspective is that the maintenance of both life and identity is accomplished through the mediation of culture. But there is no standard, accepted definition of culture in anthropology, although, as I will argue, there are certain features of the concept that are accepted by all anthropologists. If you know what an anthropologist means by culture, then you know which area or areas of the anthropological domain of inquiry he or she wishes to consider.

Anthropology began with a definition of culture, proposed by Edward B. Tylor (1973:63; originally 1871), that envisioned culture as the totality of human experience: "Culture or Civilization, taken in its wide ethnographic sense, is that complex whole which includes knowledge, belief, art, morals, law, custom, and any other capabilities and habits acquired by man as a member of society." The laundry-list approach to the concept of culture was dominant in anthropology for more than a half century following the appearance of Tylor's *Primitive Culture*. Thus Lowie (1937:253), who asserted that the "theoretical aim [of anthropology] must be to know all cultures with equal thoroughness," applied the concept of culture to a wide range of human phenomena: "[Culture is] the sum total of what an individual acquires from his society—those beliefs, customs, artistic norms, food-habits, and crafts which come to him [or her] . . . as a legacy from the past, conveyed by formal or informal education" (ibid.:3).

Even in Lowie's time, however, the use of the term *culture* was becoming less and less standard among anthropologists. In the early 1950s, Alfred Kroeber and Clyde Kluckhohn compiled a list of definitions that anthropologists through the first half of the twentieth century had offered for the concept of culture. Kroeber and Kluckhohn reprinted 164 definitions of culture, grouped into six categories: descriptive, historical, normative, psychological, structural, and genetic (Kroeber and Kluckhohn 1963; originally 1952). Counting the definitions mentioned in footnotes and other references, the authors estimated that they had identified close to three hundred different notions as to what anthropologists had in mind when they used the term *culture*.

At the time Kroeber and Kluckhohn were writing, there was an ineffectual debate in anthropology about whether "culture" properly denoted an abstraction or a tangible aspect of reality. Leslie White (1954:462) correctly noted that the debate was misconceived: "Culture . . . is a word that we may use to label a class of phenomena—things and events—in the external world." Whether or not any particular definition of culture is worthwhile or appropriate depends upon whether that definition is useful in the identification, analysis, and explanation of human phenomena. White's preference for defining culture in terms of concrete, objective, observable events and entities reflected his preoccupation with the maintenance of human life and his interest in explaining the evolution of sociocultural systems.

In the 1950s and 1960s, anthropologists began to recognize that the lack of consensus regarding the concept of culture threatened to seriously handicap the unity, identity, and effectiveness of the discipline, especially if the concept was to be the essential ingredient of a shared anthropological perspective intended to unite anthropologists of varying paradigmatic persuasions. Writing twenty years after Leslie White, Keesing (1974:73) observed that "the challenge in recent years has been to narrow the concept of 'culture' so that it includes less and reveals more." Predictably, however, the various attempts that have been made to narrow the concept of culture have fragmented rather than unified the discipline.

Keesing (1974:74–79) identifies four recent approaches to the problem of culture. The first approach regards culture as an *adaptive system* of learned beliefs and behaviors whose primary function is to adjust human societies to their environments. That approach is associated with cultural ecology and cultural materialism and can be found reflected in the work of such influential figures as Julian Steward (1955), Leslie White (1949; 1959), and Marvin Harris (1968; 1979). (The concept of culture as an adaptive system has become firmly established in contemporary archeology and is evident in the work of Lewis Binford [1962; 1968a] and Kent Flannery [1968], among many others.)

The second of the four approaches identified by Keesing views culture as a *cognitive system* composed of whatever one would need to know in order to operate in a manner acceptable to the culture's native members. That approach is associated with the paradigm known variously as ethnoscience, cognitive anthropology, or the new ethnography (see Sturtevant 1964). Its principal proponents include Harold Conklin (1955), Ward Goodenough (1956; 1964), and Charles Frake (1964a; 1964b).

The third approach regards culture as a *structural system* of shared symbols that has its analogue in the structure of the human mind. That approach is characteristic of structuralism, the paradigm created by Claude Levi-Strauss (1963; 1969a).

The fourth and final approach to the discipline's pivotal concept among contemporary anthropologists views culture as a *symbolic system* made up of shared, identifiable, public symbols and meanings. That approach is associated with the paradigm known as symbolic anthropology, which is outlined in the work of Clifford Geertz (1973; 1983) and David Schneider (1968).

Keesing concludes that there are essentially two approaches to the concept of culture among contemporary anthropologists: those that define culture in terms of both thought and behavior (the "adaptive" approaches) and those that define culture in terms of thought alone (the "ideational" approaches). Logically, of course, two additional approaches are possible: those that regard culture as composed of neither thought nor behavior and those that regard culture as composed of behavior alone. No one has suggested seriously the first possibility; indeed, it is difficult to even imagine what a culture that consisted of neither thought nor behavior could possibly be. The notion that culture consists of behavior alone has not been seriously proposed either, although the interactional approach suggested by Chapple and Arensberg comes close (Chapple and Arensberg 1940; Arensberg 1972). But as Robert Murphy (1980:45–50) explains, no purely behavioral definition of culture is supportable. All human behavior cannot be cultural behavior; if it were, there would be little point in attaching the label *cultural* to it. No purely statistical and behavioral definition of culture is possible, unless we choose to regard all abnormal behavior as noncultural behavior and ignore the fact that much abnormal behavior conforms to cultural expectations.

Other anthropologists besides Keesing have seen the contemporary controversy about the concept of culture in terms of the thought versus behavior issue. The most persistent critic of the so-called "ideational" approach to culture has been Marvin Harris (1975; 1980). Harris links the historical separation between social and cultural anthropology to the development of a purely ideational view of culture. As he describes it, ethnoscientists and others who call themselves "cultural anthropologists" are interested in the study of cognitive entities and reserve the term *social anthropology* for the statistical study of patterned social events. According to Harris (1980:392), however, it is difficult if not impossible to find anyone who is performing the valuable mission of "social anthropology": "This imaginary social anthropology has been created to avoid the onus of professional irrelevance implicit in an anthropology [i.e., "cultural anthropology"] that cannot deal with the material, concrete, historical, behavioral and 'etic' regularities of sociocultural life." For Harris (1985a:114), cultural anthropology should be concerned not with "all the rules that one must know in order to act like a native" (the ethnoscientists' view of culture), but with "the total socially acquired life-style of a group of people including patterned, repetitive ways of thinking, feeling, and acting."

If we look at the explicit definition of culture that recent anthropologists have offered, however, there is no clear consensus on the thought versus behavior issue, although purely ideational definitions of culture do appear to be relatively rare. The *Encyclopedia of Anthropology*, for example, defines culture as "the patterned behavior learned by each individual from the day of birth" (Hunter and Whitten 1976:103). Kaplan and Manners (1972:3) also advocate a definition of culture that emphasizes learned behavior: "Anthropologists are concerned not simply with human behavior but with *traditional* or *institutionalized* human behavior" (emphasis in original). But contemporary textbooks vary widely with respect to the concept of culture. Keesing (1981:509) glosses culture as "the system of knowledge more or less shared by members of a society." Aceves and King (1979:542) define culture as "learned human behavior that is transmitted down the generations." Kottak (1987:36) describes culture as "customary beliefs and behavior acquired by people as members of society." Other textbooks offer highly ambiguous definitions that fail to specify whether culture is thought or behavior or both. According to Oliver (1981:390), for example, culture is "the design for living or way of life characteristic of a hominid society."

The point I wish to make is that a good deal of ambiguity about the terms *thought* and *behavior* surrounds the debate about the ontological status of culture. When anthropologists say that culture consists of "learned and shared behavior," they hardly are excluding the cognitive aspects of cultural transmission, retention, and identification from their definitions; behavior is learned and shared precisely because it is known and thought about (and, perhaps most importantly, talked about). Similarly, when symbolic anthropologists say that systems of meaning are public, they mean that culture is expressed behaviorally and recognized in linguistic performance, body posture, ritual activity, artistic expression, and other observable human actions. Upon close examination, virtually all definitions of culture embody, as Murphy (1980:240) argues they should, some synthesis of thought and behavior.

Keesing is correct in noting that there are essentially two approaches to the concept of culture among contemporary anthropologists, but he oversimplifies the matter when he distinguishes the two approaches according to their behavioral or mental emphases. The important distinctions lie elsewhere. The adaptive approaches regard culture as a *sociocultural system* composed of behaviors and their attendant beliefs, while the ideational approaches regard culture as a *symbolic system* composed of beliefs and their attendant behaviors. Sociocultural systems are made up of the routinized, adaptive, patterned forms of interaction among the members of a society—forms of interaction that are supported, rationalized, and transmitted by shared beliefs and perspectives. Symbolic systems are made up of learned, shared, patterned sets of meanings that enable people to perceive, interpret, and evaluate life—sets of meanings that are both explicit and implicit and that are embodied and expressed in both beliefs and behaviors. Symbolic systems thus are subsets of sociocultural systems. All anthropologists recognize the existence of both sociocultural systems and symbolic systems; indeed, there is considerable precedent for the kind of conceptual distinction I am making here (see, for example, Binford 1968b).

Should we use "culture" to refer to sociocultural systems, or should we reserve the term to refer simply to symbolic systems? If we agree that both sociocultural systems and symbolic systems exist, then the debate is largely a semantic one. Lawless (1979:48) suggests that "culture may be . . . defined as the learned, rational, integrated, shared, [symbol-mediated] patterns of behavior and beliefs that are dynamically adaptive and that depend on human social interaction for their existence." I suggest that is a basic concept with which all anthropologists would agree and that this concept lies at the heart of the anthropological perspective. In the interests of conceptual clarity, anthropologists would do well to adopt a consistent definition of culture. The symbolic anthropologists have a strong argument in their favor for calling symbolic systems "culture" and sociocultural systems "sociocultural systems"—after all, it is the human capacity for symbolic communication (read "culture") that distinguishes human sociocultural systems from other primate social systems.

At this juncture, however, it seems unlikely that those who wish to call sociocultural systems "culture" will willingly abandon the term. Given the fact that the controversy is essentially semantic, there seems little point in insisting they should. As long as the term *culture* is used clearly, it is not essential that it be used consistently. It is merely essential that anthropologists specify whether they mean sociocultural system or symbolic system when they use the term *culture*. For the sake of convenience, culture will be used in this book to refer to sociocultural systems because that is the more comprehensive of the two definitions.

Whether they mean sociocultural systems or symbolic systems when they use the term, all anthropologists agree about the pervasiveness and significance of culture. Hall (1966:177) writes that "no matter how hard man tries it is impossible for him to divest himself of his own culture, for it has penetrated to the roots of his nervous system and determines how he perceives the world." He says further that *"people cannot act or interact at all in any meaningful way except through the medium of culture"* (ibid.; emphasis in original). This is the point lost on most other social scientists (including psychologists, sociologists, and economists) who uncritically base their investigations upon the foundations of their own cultural assumptions. Anthropologists cannot avoid referring to the concept of culture when explaining the human condition.

In summary, I have identified the scientific approach as the epistemological foundation of anthropology; I have described the origins, consequences, and implications of human efforts to maintain life and identity as the domain of anthropological inquiry; and I have pointed to the existence of culture as the fundamental ontological and theoretical assumption of the anthropological enterprise. Given these conclusions, certain implications follow for the pursuit of anthropological inquiry. All human beings perceive and understand the world through the medium of their culture, and anthropologists are no exception. But anthropologists claim to be scientists whose understanding of the world is objective, accurate, and reliable. Accordingly, anthropologists (like all social scientists) are faced with the task of distinguishing, in some meaningful way, between culturally specific knowledge about the human condition and objectively valid knowledge pertinent to the domain of anthropological inquiry. In the past quarter-century, anthropologists have attempted to apply the concept of the emic/etic distinction to that task. Emics and etics, then, demand careful analysis.

Suggestions for Further Reading

The Concept of Culture, by Robert Lawless (1979), is an excellent introduction to the discipline's pivotal concept. *Culture: A Critical Review of Concepts and Definitions,* by Kroeber and Kluckhohn, (1963; originally 1952) is of course somewhat dated, but it is still one of the most comprehensive treatments of the topic. Roger Keesing's (1974) review article, "Theories of Culture," is worth careful reading, as is Robert Murphy's (1980) original and thought-provoking book, *The Dialectics of Social Life.* For an intuitive appreciation of the profound significance and pervasiveness of culture, Edward Hall's (1966) *The Hidden Dimension* is invaluable.

7

The Importance of the Emic/Etic Distinction

Most introductory textbooks in anthropology describe the discipline as "holistic" and "comparative." The anthropological perspective is holistic because it tries to examine the whole of human experience. That is, unlike political scientists, sociologists, or economists, anthropologists try to look beyond political, social, or economic behavior to the interplay among all these factors of human life and to see the connections between them. Of course, anthropologists attempt to incorporate many more factors into their "holistic" analyses, including biological, ecological, linguistic, historical, and ideological variables. The anthropological perspective is comparative because it seeks its information and tests its explanations among all of the prehistorical, historical, and contemporary cultures to which anthropologists have access.

The anthropological approach may not always be holistic and comparative in practice, but anthropology is the only discipline among the social sciences that has established holism and comparison as ideals to be pursued. As a result, anthropology has been the only social science to be systematically concerned with the distinction between emic and etic knowledge.

The distinction between emics and etics is analogous to the distinction between phonemics and phonetics; the linguist Kenneth Pike (1967), in fact, derived the terms *emic* and *etic* from that analogy. Very simply, emic refers to the native's viewpoint; etic refers to the scientist's viewpoint. Emic constructs are descriptions and analyses conducted in terms of the conceptual schemes and categories considered meaningful by the participants in the event or situation being described and analyzed. Etic constructs are descriptions and analyses conducted in terms of the conceptual schemes and categories considered meaningful by the community of scientific observers.

In a brief but well-conceived introduction to anthropological theory, Robert Lawless (1979) eschews the terms *emic* and *etic* in favor of the terms *folk model* and *analytic model*. Folk models, according to Lawless, are the stereotypical, normative, uncritical representations of reality shared by the members of a given culture. Analytic models, on the other hand, are the processional, explanatory, comprehensive representations of reality recognized by the scientific community. The distinction Lawless makes between folk and analytic models is identical to the one I think should be made between emics and etics. Indeed, I would be quite willing to use the terminology that Lawless proposes were it not for the fact that the terms *emic* and *etic* already have become established in the anthropological literature.

Having said that, however, I hasten to note that the terms have been the object of nearly as much semantic discussion and debate as has the concept of culture. Various anthropologists have accused each other of using "emic" and "etic" in an "incorrect" fashion. I see little to be gained by joining in the debate about the "correct" use of a neologism with no established, standard usage or application. I would rather attempt to formulate, from a synthesis of the extant literature, a set of precise and productive definitions.

It is difficult to skirt the emic/etic controversy entirely, however, and it will be necessary first to say what emics and etics are not. Emics and etics have nothing to do with ontological issues. Events, situations, relationships, and facts are never either emic or etic. It is possible to speak of emic *descriptions*, or etic *analyses*, or even emic or etic *explanations*, but it is not possible to speak of emic or etic *things*. Events and entities that belong to the empirical world are simply events and entities; their ontological status remains unchanged whether they are referred to as "emic" or "etic" because emics and etics are first, last, and always epistemological constructs. Whether a particular description, analysis, explanation, or claim to knowledge is emic or etic must be established solely on epistemological grounds.

Marvin Harris has long been among the leading proponents of the emic/etic distinction in anthropological research. I do not agree with many of his conclusions about the implications of emics and etics (as I will explain in Chapter 10), but I do believe that he has offered a useful means of distinguishing between emic and etic statements on an epistemological basis.

> Emic operations have as their hallmark the elevation of the native informant to the status of ultimate judge of the adequacy of the observer's descriptions and analyses. The test of the adequacy of emic analyses is their ability to generate statements the native accepts as real, meaningful or appropriate. . . . Etic operations have as their hallmark the elevation of observers to the status of ultimate judges of the categories and concepts used in description and analysis (Harris 1979:32).

Although emics and etics are epistemological constructs, they are concerned not with the method of inquiry, but with the structure of inquiry. That is to say, the critical epistemological test is not how the knowledge is obtained, but how it is validated. It is possible to frame questions in such a way as to obtain etic interpretations from native informants, just as it is possible to obtain emic interpretations of events by the independent observation of those events (or at least to make reasonable predictions of emic responses based upon independent observations). The distinction between elicitation and observation is not by itself sufficient to establish the emic or etic status of descriptions and analyses. Instead, those descriptions and analyses must be measured against other standards—namely, the judgment of natives (for emics) and the evaluation of scientists (for etics).

An illustration may be helpful here. In the course of fieldwork on Virgin Gorda in the British Virgin Islands, I observed local reaction to media reports of rising crime rates on nearby islands (particularly Tortola and St. Thomas). I observed, on repeated occasions, the stunned, silent reactions of native inhabitants to radio news stories describing homicides and other crimes of personal violence. I knew, based upon police reports and personal observation, that crimes of personal violence were all but unknown on Virgin Gorda. I knew, too, that Virgin Gorda's small population, rural settlement pattern, diffuse social controls, and extensive kin networks all mitigated against the incidence of local crime. Based upon those observations, I inferred that Virgin Gordians would be likely to express confusion and bewilderment at the thought of violent crime. (That inference, of course, was based upon my knowledge of Virgin

Gordian culture and my understanding of the characteristic attitudes of Virgin Gordians.) In short, I offered an emic description of native thought regarding crime (Lett 1981). What made my description emic, however, was not the method by which the knowledge was obtained, or the fact that the description applied to the world view of the participants, but the fact that I subsequently checked my inferences with my informants and confirmed that they considered my statements to be real, appropriate, and accurate representations of their attitudes and perceptions.

In testing my inferences with my informants, I did not ask simply, "Would you say that you are bewildered and confused by the crime reports?" (Bewilderment and confusion, after all, could be categories appropriate to my culture but not to theirs.) Instead, I asked open-ended questions—"What do you think about that?"—and listened carefully to the responses. When the islanders said, "We don't understand how a man could do that to another man. It's horrible. It's unthinkable," I concluded that my characterization of their perceptions—of the emic perception in this case—was accurate.

Etic knowledge is validated in an analogous fashion. For an etic description or analysis to be recognized as etic, it must be accepted by the scientific community as an appropriate and meaningful account. Harris (1976:341) notes that "when the description is responsive to the observer's categories of time, place, weights and measure, actor types, numbers of people present, body motion, and environmental effect, it is etic." To be etic, terms, categories, concepts, and units of measurement must have a precise, unambiguous, recognized (or recognizable) meaning within the scientific community.

In the interest of formulating a precise definition of the term, I would suggest that anthropological accounts and explanations are etic if they satisfy the following four criteria:

1. The accounts must be considered meaningful and appropriate by the worldwide community of scientific observers. This is not simply a criterion of consensus. It means that the terms and concepts employed must satisfy the scientific ideals of precision, reliability, and accuracy. (Emic accounts, of course, are validated by consensus—the consensus of native informants.)

2. The accounts must be validated (or validatable) by independent observers. This means that the procedures employed in the formulation of etic descriptions must be replicable by independent observers and that independent observers must be able to obtain the same test results when attempting to validate etic accounts.

3. The accounts must satisfy the canons of scientific knowledge and evidence. This means that etic accounts, analyses, and explanations must be falsifiable and that they must not be contradicted by other available

evidence. All available evidence must be considered in the formulation of etic accounts. (These same criteria apply when evaluating the authenticity of emic accounts—that is, it is necessary to demonstrate, in a falsifiable fashion, that a given emic account truly enjoys the consensus of native informants.)

4. The accounts must be applicable cross-culturally. This is a necessary but not sufficient condition for etic constructs. It means that etic accounts must not be dependent upon particular, local frames of reference; these accounts must be generalizable. This criterion is intended to ensure that scientists will consider whether their supposedly etic constructs and the tests used to validate those constructs might be dependent upon emic assumptions. For example, many contemporary psychologists subscribe to "developmental stages theory" and offer explanations that refer to "midlife crises" resulting from "career dissatisfaction" (see Erikson 1959; Feibleman 1975; Sheehy 1976; Stevenson 1977; Gould 1978; Stevens-Long 1979; Hultsch and Deutsch 1981). Those concepts are not etic unless people in all cultures pass through the same developmental stages (which is untrue), or unless developmental stages are shown to be particular cultural manifestations of larger pancultural processes (which psychologists have yet to do).

The works on developmental stages theory cited here all illustrate the dangers that beset social scientists who fail to maintain a rigorous distinction between emics and etics. Each of these books bears the superficial imprimatur of science; each is written by a credentialed expert affiliated with an accredited institution of higher learning; each is avowedly based upon social scientific research; yet each is scarcely more than the emics of U.S. middle-class culture dressed in the jargon of contemporary psychology. Each is thoroughly ethnocentric. None of the authors evidences more than a passing acquaintance with the fact that different cultures divide the human life cycle differently; all seem to assume that the "developmental stages" functional in their own culture (for example, high school graduation as a point of demarcation for the passage to adulthood) are the same for all people in all places in all times. No social science can ignore the emic/etic distinction and claim any legitimacy for its explanations.

These four criteria for etic accounts leave open the possibility that native informants may possess etic knowledge, as is sometimes the case. The emic or etic status of any particular claim to knowledge is not dependent upon the origin of that knowledge. These criteria also preclude the possibility of legitimate criticism from those who claim that anthropological etics are no more than the emics of Western culture. Anthropological etics are more valuable than native emics (for certain tasks) because they are more epistemologically responsible. This does not mean, however, that etic knowledge is the only appropriate goal of anthropological research. Whether emic or etic knowledge is desirable depends upon the question at hand (see Pelto and Pelto 1978).

Without a rigorous emic/etic distinction, it is impossible to tell whether the explanations offered by social scientists are different in kind from the explanations offered by other people. As anthropologists, our claims to privileged, valid, reliable explanations rest upon our pursuit of etic knowledge. Although it is possible to give either scientific or nonscientific descriptions, accounts, and comparisons in either emic or etic terms, scientific explanations must be etic explanations. We can and should describe emics from a scientific perspective, and such descriptions often are necessary for scientific analysis (they are certainly necessary for cultural translation). If we wish to explain the human condition, however, we ultimately must make reference not to what particular groups of people think and feel about their experiences, but to the actual, objective attributes of the human condition.

The familiar arguments against such an objective understanding of the human condition (or any aspect of the universe) are not episte-mologically responsible. Granted, "objective" reality depends upon the theories that guide its perception, and, granted, those theories are dependent upon a host of factors, including the attributes of the human sensory apparatus and the prejudices of the human investigator. Granted, too, the tests that we devise to validate our claims to etic knowledge are not always valid tests of the claims we hope to establish. But these are all practical problems that in principle can be overcome. There is order and regularity in the world; no one can reasonably doubt that. There is no logical reason why we cannot apprehend the order in human affairs. By establishing etic knowledge as an ideal, anthropologists insist that anthropological knowledge must be self-correcting. Our claims to objective knowledge about the human condition are justified by our continuing, cumulative efforts to test every claim to knowledge. We regard etic knowledge as objectively valid knowledge precisely because we regard it as tentative knowledge. If an account claims to be etic (or, for that matter, emic), it is never immune from relentless scrutiny.

Etic knowledge, then, is an ideal, but it is an ideal against which all other explanations of the human condition must be measured. No other standard yet developed for the analysis of human affairs incorporates a self-correcting guard against ethnocentric bias. No other standard yet developed takes account of the incontrovertible fact that different cultures have different understandings of the world.

In one respect at least, the social sciences are different from the natural sciences. Anthropologists face practical problems that do not concern astronomers, geologists, and physicists—unlike stars, rocks, and atoms, human beings study themselves. All human beings hold theories about the nature of humanity; the overwhelming majority of people hold nothing more than culturally specific theories. If we are to investigate scientifically the human condition, we must distinguish between those theories that we hold as enculturated individuals and those theories that we hold as scientists. Any social science that fails to make that distinction is not social nor is it scientific.

One last thing remains to be said about the anthropological perspective. There is an unavoidably human dimension to anthropological inquiry because anthropology is practiced by anthropologists. As a distinct subculture, the discipline of anthropology has a particular organizational structure and a particular value system. Anthropological knowledge and theory should not be evaluated apart from that context.

Suggestions for Further Reading

The original use of the terms *emic* and *etic* can be found in Kenneth Pike's (1967) book *Language in Relation to a Unified Theory of the Structures of Human Behavior*. Robert Lawless (1979) offers a clear and compelling distinction between emic and etic knowledge in *The Concept of Culture*. Marvin Harris (1979) discusses the concepts of emics and etics in depth in *Cultural Materialism*. For a summary of the major issues of the emic/etic debate, see Harris (1964; 1976), Burling (1964), Goodenough (1970), and Durbin (1972).

8

The Culture
of Anthropology

One of the most apparent features of contemporary U.S. anthropology
is its highly elaborated organizational structure. When Franz Boas helped
found the American Anthropological Association in 1902, he hardly
could have anticipated the tremendous involution (to borrow Goldenweiser's [1936] unjustly forgotten term) of anthropological associations.
Today there are scores of groups, societies, and associations that have
been established for the discipline as a whole (such as the American
Anthropological Association), for each subdiscipline (such as the American
Ethnological Society), for broad areas of research (such as the Society
for Psychological Anthropology), for narrowly defined topics of research
(such as the Society for Menstrual Cycle Research), and for geographical
areas of interest (such as the Caribbean Studies Association). There are
more than twenty anthropological journals in the mainstream of the
discipline and many times that number of journals in which anthropologists regularly publish. New journals appear every year, and the
trend is toward ever more narrow and esoteric specializations.

The elaboration of this pattern is due principally to the structure of
the U.S. university system. Despite recent changes in the job market,
most anthropologists continue to work in an academic environment,
where recognition, promotion, and tenure are dependent largely upon

scholarly production, measured in terms of the quality and quantity of publications. Journals and associations are intended to further the scientific enterprise by promoting communication among scientists, but the economic facts of academic life have created a system in which publication often becomes an end in itself. These observations are commonplace, but they have a significant import for the conduct of anthropological inquiry, as Robert Murphy (1980:vii–viii) explains: "The linked trends [in contemporary U.S. anthropology] toward miniaturization of problem and quantification of data are congruent with the rapid expansion in numbers of anthropologists, each of whom must establish a claim to a 'turf,' a domain of ideas and fieldwork which, however small, is his. More than the unity of anthropology is threatened." Among the other threats Murphy (ibid.:viii) envisions are the danger of "empirical trivialization" and the "search for brilliant solutions to squalid questions." In practice, the anthropological domain of inquiry is often defined not by sound theoretical considerations but by the exigencies of scholarly life, often in concert with contemporary fads.

There are other limitations imposed by the academic nature of the anthropological enterprise, notable among them the discipline's self-imposed barrier to communication with the general public. Anthropologists are not accustomed to sharing their insights with audiences other than those composed of their colleagues or their students, and as a result, anthropologists have ignored and been all but ignored by the most powerful and pervasive medium of mass communication in the history of the world. I have had fairly extensive experience in the electronic mass media as a radio and television journalist, and I can attest that the mutual suspicion and antipathy that characterize relations between journalists and academicians are often well founded on both sides (see Lett 1985b; 1986; 1987a; 1987b). I believe it is significant, however, that psychologists, including psychologists employed in academic environments, are much more adept at popularizing their theories through the mass media than are anthropologists, and I believe the image anthropologists present of themselves to the world at large says a good deal about the image they hold of themselves. There have been notable exceptions, of course (including Margaret Mead, Loren Eiseley, Marvin Harris, and Stephen Jay Gould), but as a discipline we have acquiesced to the public perception that anthropology is an arcane, esoteric, and largely irrelevant activity.

The definitive anthropological study of the subculture of anthropology has yet to be undertaken (see Scholte 1972), but I can offer a few preliminary observations. In addition to its distinctive organizational structure, the discipline has a distinctive set of values as well. Predictably, many of those values can be seen as a direct emanation of the structural-functional requisites of disciplinary organization. For example, professional status among anthropologists is dependent upon the successful completion of fieldwork, the sine qua non of anthropological identity, or, as Manners and Kaplan (1968:1) note, a "touchstone of adequacy, a *rite de passage* prerequisite to membership in the profession." In a brief but perceptive critique of the anthropological passion for the field experience, Salzman (1986:528) aptly observes that "more than anything else, it is ethnographic fieldwork that . . . demarcates the transition from being a student of anthropology to being an anthropologist." Intensive, lengthy, foreign fieldwork is one of the principal distinguishing features of the discipline; fieldwork is one of the characteristics that sets anthropologists apart from sociologists and psychologists, and as such it is one of the means used to validate anthropology's claim to a niche within the university system. Field research, obviously, is an indispensable part of the discipline, and it hardly could be otherwise. One of the chief merits of anthropology, in contrast with other social sciences, is that anthropological knowledge is based upon the firsthand observation of human behavior in its natural setting.

For the most part, however, anthropologists do not regard fieldwork as a mere scientific tool. In the anthropological value system, the fieldwork experience is imbued with a special significance and sanctity. Eric Wolf (1964:89) observes that "there is a sense in which, in the private ranking systems of American anthropologists, the first-class recorder of ethnographic detail ranks more highly than the most gifted theorist." Much has been written about fieldwork—its techniques, difficulties, and rewards—but much more remains to be said about the esteem anthropologists hold for the fieldwork experience. (For a list of works dealing specifically with anthropological fieldwork, see Lawless, Sutlive, and Zamora 1983.)

Nor do anthropologists regard the subjects of their field research dispassionately. At the core of the anthropological value system is an affinity and affection for the variety and diversity of cultures in the world. In a sensitive and elegant ethnography of the Tapirapé Indians, Charles Wagley (1977:304) expresses this peculiarly anthropological viewpoint: "Each human culture, in its own way, has a view of the world in its own terms and each has much to offer. And each of these small societies represents a solution by an organized human society and culture to the fundamental problems of man—human reproduction, understanding the real and imaginary forces of the universe, and achieving some measure of human well-being."

Whether any particular society has "much to offer" to the solution of universal human problems is an empirical question, and surely it is possible that some society has or has had little to contribute to that end. But I think Wagley and most anthropologists believe that the worth of particular cultures is not limited to the appropriateness of their solutions to the quandary of human existence. Most anthropologists hold that different cultures are valuable simply because they are different. That may well be an entirely defensible value position, but it is a value position nonetheless. It is a value further reflected in the "Principles of Professional Responsibility" adopted by the American Anthropological Association in 1971 (reprinted in Rynkiewich and Spradley 1976:183–186), which affirm that an anthropologist's primary ethical responsibility is to the people he or she studies.

An important corollary to that value can be found in the doctrine of cultural relativism, which, depending on your perspective, is either the most famous or the most infamous of all anthropological values. In its simplest, purest, and most defensible expression, cultural relativism maintains that the beliefs and behaviors of another culture should not be evaluated according to the standards of one's own culture, but should instead be evaluated relative to the culture of which they are a part. In other words, cultural relativism is simply the obverse of ethnocentrism. The implications of the doctrine, however, have been criticized roundly by philosophers, anthropologists, and others who insist that there must be ethical standards of human conduct that are applicable cross-culturally. If no such standards exist, we immediately encounter major ethical dilemmas as we pursue cultural relativism to its logical conclusion— for example, are we forced to accept the atrocities of Nazi Germany on the grounds that those atrocities were part and parcel of German culture in the 1930s and 1940s?

The answer must be no, and that is the answer given even by anthropologists who do subscribe to the doctrine of cultural relativism. Those anthropologists, however, are vulnerable to the charge of logical inconsistency. Elvin Hatch has suggested a solution to the ethical and philosophical problems arising from the doctrine of cultural relativism. He advocates that anthropologists adopt instead a more sophisticated "humanistic principle"—one he claims is not culture-bound, one that would aver that "the well-being of people ought to be respected" (Hatch 1983:134). At this time, there does not seem to be a clear consensus whether anthropologists are willing to abandon their long-cherished cultural relativism for Hatch's humanistic principle, but it is clear that anthropologists share a strong conviction that ethnocentrism is insidious, which is significant. The fear of ethnocentrism is not something that troubles doctors or lawyers or even psychologists, but it is an abiding concern among anthropologists.

That fear of ethnocentrism can have peculiar consequences. Anthropologists, it seems to me, have a tendency to retreat so far from xenophobia that they display at times what might be called ethnophobia, or a fear of their own culture. When I was a graduate student at the University of Florida in the early 1980s, most students in the department were very unlikely to make prejudicial or stereotypical remarks about ethnic minorities or peasants, yet many of them frequently offered disparaging comments about "preppies" and "yuppies." Certainly those remarks were generally facetious, or at least ostensibly so, but I think it is fair to say that most anthropologists have more sympathy and affection for the downtrodden and disenfranchised inhabitants of the Third World than they do for the affluent and powerful members of the U.S. upper middle class.

In a similar way, I think anthropologists tend to be more distrustful and suspicious of the received wisdom of their own cultures than they are of the beliefs, values, and attitudes of other cultures. In *The Anthropological Imagination*, Muriel Dimen-Schein (1977:xii) confesses a very personal motivation for her commitment to anthropology: "I was drawn to its moral emphasis that our own culture was not the best or only way to live, and that alternatives existed. I found this debunking deeply satisfying, given my profoundly unsatisfying adolescence in the suburban conformist culture of the late 1950s." I would not be surprised if many U.S. anthropologists were to recognize something of themselves in that. As the son of a career military officer I spent several of my formative years living overseas, and by an early age I had come to view my own culture from an expatriate's perspective. As an undergraduate majoring in anthropology at the College of William and Mary in the mid-1970s, I was not alone. Many of my fellow students were the offspring of professional soldiers, diplomats, international business executives, and missionaries. My own experience leads me to suspect that many anthropologists may have been forged in the youthful experience of cross-cultural contact.

What I do know with certainty is that the anthropological value system, like any other, is promulgated in regular interaction. Any anthropologist who has ever attended an annual meeting of the American Anthropological Association knows what Anthony Wallace (1966) means by a rite of social intensification. Despite the fact that there are scores and scores of seminars, symposia, and speeches at every session—where hundreds and hundreds of papers are delivered, discussed, and debated— the real work of the annual ritual goes on in the corridors, cocktail lounges, and coffee klatsches of the convention center where anthropologists meet and greet one another, solicit jobs and grants, reaffirm their solidarity, and rededicate themselves to a shared value system.

I do not pretend that I have done more than sketch the broad outlines of that value system, and I realize that many will find my characterization too impressionistic. I will grant that criticism in advance. I simply mean to suggest that anthropologists tend to share a particular set of preconceptions and preferences and that those perspectives influence what anthropologists choose to study and how and why they study it. Fashions and fads play a role in academe just as they do in popular culture. None of this necessarily detracts from the scientific validity of anthropology. In fact, fads normally play a fairly minimal role, but this role should not be ignored.

We come now to the less general and more specific part of the book. In discussing "the anthropological perspective" I have tried to summarize the essential characteristics of the discipline. I have described anthropology as a scientific approach to the study of the human condition, and I have argued that the concept of culture and the notion of the emic/etic distinction are the fundamental theoretical perspectives that distinguish anthropology from the other social sciences. To this point, then, I have laid the groundwork for an analysis of particular anthropological theories. In Part 1, I explained that scientific inquiry is paradigmatic. In Part 2, I argued that anthropological inquiry is scientific. It follows that anthropological inquiry must be paradigmatic. Part 3 explores the implications of that conclusion.

Suggestions for Further Reading

For a discussion of the value anthropologists hold for fieldwork, see Philip Salzman's (1986) essay in *Current Anthropology*; a comprehensive list of sources can be found in *Fieldwork: The Human Experience*, edited by Lawless, Sutlive, and Zamora (1983). For a thorough discussion of the concept of cultural relativism, see Elvin Hatch's (1983) *Culture and Morality*. U.S. anthropologists lately have become much more interested in the study of their own culture; for a sample of that work, see the review article by George and Louise Spindler (1983) in *Annual Reviews in Anthropology* and the collection of articles in *Symbolizing America*, edited by Hervé Varenne (1986).

PART THREE

THE WISDOM
OF ECLECTICISM

*In order to be coherent, it is not
necessary to carry a banner.*
—Reuben Abel
Man Is the Measure

9

The Range
of Alternatives

All anthropological research is conducted under the auspices of some particular paradigm. Nonparadigmatic research is a contradiction in terms because the activity of research necessarily involves the definition of a research problem and the identification of an appropriate means of solving that problem. Not all research is explicitly paradigmatic, however. In the conduct of scientific inquiry, scientists frequently are vague about the sources of their theories and inspirations. Conscious deliberation does not always guide the selection of paradigms. Inconsistency often characterizes the manner in which various paradigms are applied to various problems, and, of course, paradigms range from the amorphous to the precise.

Anthropologists are faced with the task of building a scientific understanding of the human experience that is comprehensive and progressive. That task has two parts: first, the construction of meaningful and productive paradigms capable of explaining significant human phenomena, and second, the refinement of those paradigms based upon critical and comparative analysis. The comparison of paradigms inevitably leads to the selection of paradigms, as some paradigms will be replaced by other more attractive paradigms. Ultimately, the goal of the anthropological enterprise is to develop ever more precise and parsimonious paradigms that account for the human condition in an ever more cogent fashion. There probably will not ever be a best paradigm, however; at most, any paradigm only can be better than its extant rivals because no paradigm ever could address all possible questions.

This history of anthropology has been one of growing theoretical divergence, and that pattern continues today. There is no general agreement as to the number of paradigms in contemporary anthropology, but there is general agreement, as Barrett (1984:xii) observes, that the discipline is "multiparadigmatic." It undoubtedly is true, as Malefijt (1977:255) says, that "the profusion of theories has often befuddled the general public and the beginning student alike." I do not intend to provide a detailed or comprehensive review and analysis of every anthropological paradigm that exists or ever has existed. Instead, I have selected three paradigms for close scrutiny to illustrate the principles of paradigmatic evaluation outlined in Chapter 3, but I will reserve that discussion for Chapters 10, 11, and 12. In this chapter, I want to list briefly what are widely regarded as the most influential paradigms of the past century, and then I want to consider the question of which paradigm is most popular today.

For additional details about each of the following paradigms, see the suggested readings listed at the end of this chapter. These thumbnail sketches only are intended to identify each paradigm's domain of inquiry.

Anthropological Paradigms

Classical Evolutionism. This paradigm developed in the late nineteenth century when the discipline was first acquiring a distinct identity. The classical evolutionists—most notably Lewis Henry Morgan (1877) and Edward B. Tylor (1871)—sought to trace the development of human culture from its earliest, primitive beginnings to its latest, most complex form (namely, nineteenth century Western civilization). The paradigm was handicapped by a reliance on secondhand data, an implicit ethnocentrism, and a tendency to generate speculative and untestable theories. However, classical evolutionism was responsible for the development of the comparative method, which has proven an enduring contribution to anthropology.

Diffusionism. This paradigm, especially popular in Great Britain and Germany in the early twentieth century, was concerned primarily with explaining the similarities among different cultures. Diffusion is an historical process of cultural change involving the cross-cultural transmission of material objects and learned behaviors and beliefs. The most notable of the European diffusionists were Fritz Graebner (1911) and

Father Wilhelm Schmidt (1939). In the United States, this paradigm found expression in the "culture area" school and was reflected most prominently in the work of Clark Wissler (1917) and Alfred Kroeber (1939). Diffusionism has not had any significant proponents since the middle of the twentieth century (Broce 1973:37).

Historical Particularism. This paradigm, founded by the father of U.S. anthropology, Franz Boas (1963; originally 1911), was concerned primarily with the collection of ethnographic data and the description of particular cultures. Historical particularists rejected the sometimes speculative theories of the classical evolutionists and instead sought to identify the historical processes responsible for the development of particular cultures. Historical particularists stressed the importance of extensive firsthand field research; their goal was to make as complete and as accurate a record as possible of the life ways of native peoples. Historical particularism has left an indelible imprint on U.S. anthropology. However, virtually no anthropological research is conducted now under the auspices of the paradigm; the significance of historical particularism is exclusively historical.

Structural-Functionalism. This paradigm was developed primarily in Great Britain, principally by A. R. Radcliffe-Brown (1952) and Bronislaw Malinowski (1922). The paradigm's underlying principle is a biological analogy: Structural-functionalism assumes that the components of social systems, like the body parts of an organism, function to maintain the integrity and stability of the entire system. In the United States, the paradigm achieved its greatest impact among sociologists, of whom Talcott Parsons (1937) was the most important. Structural-functionalism inspires little if any anthropological research today, even though the concept of function is implicit in all anthropological theories about the structure of societies.

Psychological Anthropology. This paradigm, first developed in the United States in the 1920s, was originally called "culture and personality." Psychological anthropology addresses itself to three broad topics: the relationship between culture and human nature; the relationship between culture and individual personality; and the relationship between culture and a society's typical personality type. Research in psychological anthropology relies heavily upon concepts and techniques developed in psychology (see Campbell and Naroll 1972). The two key figures in the origin of the paradigm were Margaret Mead (1928) and Ruth Benedict (1934). The paradigm continues to be influential today.

Structuralism. This paradigm is the brainchild of French anthropologist Claude Levi-Strauss (1963; 1976). Structuralism is a research strategy for uncovering the structure of the human mind—that is, the structure of human thought processes—which structuralists say is the same cross-culturally. Structuralism assumes that human thought always is structured in terms of binary oppositions, and structuralists claim that those oppositions are reflected in a variety of cultural phenomena, including language, mythology, kinship, and cuisine. This paradigm will be reviewed thoroughly in Chapter 11.

Dialectical Materialism. The fundamental theoretical principles of this paradigm were first articulated by Karl Marx (Marx and Engels 1948; originally 1848) more than a century ago. Dialectical materialists attempt to explain the reasons for the change and development of sociocultural systems. Proponents of the paradigm maintain that a society's structure and ideology are determined by its mode of production and believe that capitalist societies contain the seeds of their own destruction in the inherent "contradiction" between the desire for profit and the need to exploit labor (Godelier 1977). Many contemporary anthropologists have been inspired by the paradigm, including Marshall Sahlins (1976b). For a well-conceived critique of dialectical materialism, see Harris (1979:141–164).

Cultural Materialism. This paradigm attempts to explain the causes of sociocultural similarities and differences. In its earliest formulation, as developed by Leslie White (1949; 1959) and Julian Steward (1955), it was known as "neoevolutionism" or "cultural ecology"; now the paradigm is most closely associated with the work of Marvin Harris (1979). Cultural materialists maintain that a society's modes of production and reproduction determine its social structure and ideological superstructure, but cultural materialists reject the metaphysical notion of Hegelian dialectics that is part of dialectical materialism. The paradigm of cultural materialism will be the subject of Chapter 10.

Ethnoscience. This paradigm is also known as "cognitive anthropology" or the "new ethnography." It was developed in the United States in the 1950s and 1960s as a research strategy for identifying the implicit cultural rules that underlie behavior (see Tyler 1969). The fundamental theoretical perspective of the paradigm is embodied in the notion of componential analysis, which holds that components of cultural categories (of color, art, flora and fauna, the supernatural realm, and so on) can be analyzed in their own terms to see how the culture structures its field of cognition (the assumption being that the cognitive structures of different cultures are different and ultimately untranslatable). The paradigm's principal architects include Harold Conklin (1955; 1969), Ward Goodenough (1956), and Charles Frake (1964a; 1969). In *Cultural Materialism*, Harris (1979:265–286) does a good job of pointing out the theoretical deficiencies of ethnoscience.

Symbolic Anthropology. This paradigm is founded upon the assumption that human beings are quintessentially meaning-seeking animals, and it seeks to explore the various symbolic ways in which individual human beings, and cultural groups of human beings, assign meaning to their lives. Also called "interpretive anthropology," the paradigm is associated primarily with the work of Clifford Geertz (1973; 1983). This paradigm will be examined closely in Chapter 12.

Sociobiology. This paradigm is characterized as "biological reductionism" by most sociocultural anthropologists and embraced by only a few biological anthropologists. It was developed by a biologist, Edward Wilson (1975), who attempted to apply the principles of biological evolution to social phenomena and to explain much of cultural behavior in terms of genetic programming. For a thorough discussion of the weaknesses of sociobiological theory, see Sahlins (1976a).

We come now to the question of which of these research strategies can claim the most adherents among contemporary anthropologists. The answer is not readily apparent. If there is a predominant paradigm in anthropology today, it is elusive and difficult to identify. Some well-recognized paradigms, such as diffusionism, historical particularism, functionalism, and structural-functionalism, have all but completely lost their influence and retain only an historical significance within the discipline. Others, such as cultural materialism, structuralism, dialectical materialism, and cognitive anthropology, are undeniably influential but hardly can be said to characterize the majority of contemporary anthropological research. Still others, such as sociobiology, structural Marxism (Sahlins 1976b), and "obscurantism" (Harris 1979:315–341), are distinctly marginal and decidedly unpopular among most professional anthropologists. But if not cultural ecologists, ethnoscientists, or classical evolutionists, what then are most contemporary anthropologists?

In *Cultural Materialism,* Harris answers that the majority of his colleagues are "eclectics." Eclecticism, according to Harris (1979:289), is "strategic agnosticism"—a research strategy that assiduously avoids commitment to any particular set of epistemological or theoretical principles. Few eclectics call themselves eclectics, perhaps because Harris consistently has used the term in a derogatory sense. In *The Rise of Anthropological Theory,* for example, he described the self-conscious eclecticism of contemporary ethnological theorists as "little more than a euphemism for confusion" (Harris 1968:285).

There are two essential aspects to Harris's definition of eclecticism. First, to be eclectic is to concede "that all strategic [i.e., paradigmatic] options *might* be equally probable" (Harris 1979:289; emphasis in original). To be an eclectic anthropologist, then, precludes developing an interrelated, coherent, and parsimonious understanding of human social life. Second, eclecticism allows that "all sectors of sociocultural systems *might* be equally determinative" (ibid.; emphasis in original).

It is this indeterminate determinism that most disturbs Harris. "From the cultural materialist viewpoint, the chief vice of eclecticism is that it discourages researchers who encounter the least bit of difficulty from persisting in the attempt to identify plausible infrastructural determinants" (Harris 1979:304).

There is a certain plausibility to Harris's analysis. He is correct that avoiding deliberate commitment to any recognizable paradigm or paradigms is itself a commitment to a particular research strategy (there is no such thing as nonparadigmatic research). Most anthropologists do make use, at various times, of the theoretical principles (or at least the theories) of various paradigms. (Few U.S. anthropologists are structuralists, although many have made use of structuralist analyses and interpretations.) Perhaps most importantly, Harris also is correct in his observation that contemporary anthropology is replete with middle-range theories that are unrelated to one another by any overarching set of clear and well-formulated theoretical principles. Most anthropologists are not explicit about their paradigmatic commitment, and the resulting lack of coherence and parsimony is altogether real.

But is "eclecticism" an entirely apt characterization of the paradigm pursued by most anthropologists? I think not. Very few anthropologists could be convinced that "it cannot be foretold which strategies will be most productive in any given case" (Harris 1979:x), nor would many grant even that "all paradigms *might* be equally probable" (emphasis in original). It must be remembered that paradigms define their own problems. Before considering whether all paradigms might be equally probable, an essential question must be asked: equally probable for the solution of what problem? Given that different paradigms define different problems for investigation and specify different means of solution, it is meaningless to say that any one paradigm is "more probable" than any other. A given paradigm can be more or less probable than its competitor only if the two paradigms in question agree about the nature of the problem to be solved.

There is nothing inconsistent or improper about affirming that two paradigms might be "equally probable" for the solution of their stated problems if one paradigm is concerned with identifying the causes of sociocultural similarities and differences and the other paradigm is concerned with identifying the logic underlying particular emic typologies. All anthropologists, indeed all scientists, are eclectic in the sense that they apply different paradigms to different problems. Harris, however, seems to imply that eclectics apply different paradigms to similar problems. Most anthropologists usually are innocent of that particular indiscretion.

For example, consider sociobiology, dialectical materialism, and cultural materialism, all of which, in the broadest terms, can be said to be concerned with the same problem—namely, the determinants of cultural behavior and social institutions. Sharing a common problem, these paradigms are, in Kuhn's sense, relatively commensurable, and the efficacy of their various explanations therefore can be compared directly. Do most anthropologists concede that the principles of genetic inheritance, Hegelian dialectics, and infrastructural determinism might be equally probable guidelines for explaining the form and function of human social systems? If not, then most anthropologists cannot be called eclectics.

The second aspect of Harris's definition of eclecticism presents similar difficulties. Despite their lack of paradigmatic precision, most contemporary anthropologists do not concede that "all sectors of sociocultural systems might be equally determinative." Relatively few anthropologists are confused consistently about the nature of cultural causality. A great many anthropologists, however, fail to be concerned systematically with the question of cultural causality. When the question of the causes of sociocultural differences and similarities is addressed squarely, materialist rather than idealist explanations most frequently are adduced because materialists most frequently address questions of causality. (An illustration of the failure of nonmaterialists to recognize and address questions of causality will be presented in Chapter 15.) There may well be a few of Harris's eclectics among contemporary anthropologists, but there do not seem to be very many of them. Most sociocultural anthropologists do share a common paradigm, but I think most of the people Harris calls eclectics are actually what I would call cultural determinists.

The Paradigm of Cultural Determinism

If most anthropologists pursue research under the paradigm of cultural determinism, very few call themselves cultural determinists. The majority of anthropologists are generally comfortable operating within an unspecified and largely implicit paradigmatic framework. Like Arno Penzias, the Nobel Laureate quoted in "The Golden Marshalltown" (Kent Flannery's [1982:265] amusing and instructive parable about contemporary archeology), most anthropologists are "happily too busy *doing* science to have time to worry about philosophizing about it" (emphasis in original). Many anthropologists, I would suggest, share the intuitive suspicion that "doing science" and "philosophizing about it" are distinctly different, and perhaps even antithetical, activities. Flannery's parable is a clever and convenient illustration of that viewpoint.

"The Golden Marshalltown" tells the tale of an airborne encounter between four archeologists returning home from an annual meeting of the Society for American Archeology. Its author is a participant-observer in a witty dialogue about the nature and purpose of contemporary archeology. His three companions are the Born Again Philosopher, the Child of the Seventies, and the Old Timer.

The Born Again Philosopher had begun his career as a working archeologist interested in southwestern prehistory but had abandoned that pursuit in favor of office-bound speculations in the "philosophy of science" when his incompetence in the field began to catch up with him. "After a few years of dusty holes in hot, dreary valleys . . . he'd missed more floors than the elevator in the World Trade Center."

The Child of the Seventies is an unoriginal product of the "me generation." Self-centered and ambitious, his goals are simple: "to be famous, to be well paid, to be stroked, and to receive immediate gratification." The Child of the Seventies has mastered the academician's game. He has devised a way to have his doctoral dissertation published and republished in various guises, and he is making himself rich and famous by editing compilations of his colleagues' work.

The hero of the story is the Old Timer. The Old Timer has spent his career in the field patiently and professionally reconstructing the culture histories of prehistoric societies. The goal of archeology, he believes, is to teach the world something about its past. After all, he notes, the world could not care less about epistemology. The Old Timer has been forced into early retirement for the unfashionable sin of "believing in culture as the central paradigm in archeology." He is convinced that "culture," and not "psychological encounters" or "strategies of economic choice," provides the best explanation of human behavior. The Old Timer is not interested in paradigmatic debates about the best way to conduct science. He prefers instead to remain firmly on the ground—or, as it were, in the pit—and to specialize in the archeology of a "particular region or time period."   .

In the discussion that ensues in the cocktail lounge of the 747, the Born Again Philosopher says that he would like to establish a dialogue between archeology and philosophy. His ultimate goal is to make a contribution to philosophy, for he works on "a higher level of abstraction" than most of his colleagues. The Old Timer, on the other hand, hopes simply to make some contribution to archeology (the Child of the Seventies wants only to make some contribution to his own career). The Old Timer compares the Born Again Philosopher to the garrulous television announcers who sit high above the field and pass harsh judgment on the football players below. The announcers in the booth, like the professional "philosophers of science," offer intricate and highly abstract analyses of the activity on the ground, but, according to the Old Timer, those analyses have no theoretical or strategic impact on the game, whether the game is football or archeology. The real contributions, he observes, are made by the players and the coaches who are involved directly in the field of play.

Most anthropologists, I suspect, would be inclined to identify themselves with the Old Timer. Fieldwork is the hallmark of professionalism among cultural anthropologists just as it is among archeologists. An anthropologist's command of the ethnographic literature dealing with some particular culture area is regarded, in large part, as a measure of his or her professional competence. Most contemporary anthropologists would be more likely to define themselves as Caribbeanists or Africanists or Latin Americanists than as cultural materialists or structuralists or symbolic anthropologists, although more likely still to define themselves simply as anthropologists. As Harris (1968:284) observes, "Most anthropologists simply want to be left in peace to pursue the study of their 'people.'" Like the Old Timer, most anthropologists rely heavily upon the concept of "culture" as an explanatory mechanism.

Flannery's parable suggests that the paradigm of choice among most anthropologists is one that might be called "cultural determinism." The fundamental question posed by the paradigm of cultural determinism is this: "Why do human beings behave in different ways and hold different beliefs?" (That is a very different question than the one posed by cultural materialism, which asks instead, "Why are there different systems of behavior and beliefs in the world?")

Cultural determinism is not a well-articulated paradigm. It incorporates a number of general theoretical assumptions, but it includes few precise theoretical principles. (Principles inspire the formulation of particular theories that in turn lead to the creation of testable hypotheses, whereas theoretical assumptions are the basic ontological premises that underlie theoretical principles. Theoretical assumptions may have explanatory power in their own right, but, for the most part, they do not give rise to a wide range of more precise theories.)

One of the fundamental theoretical assumptions of cultural determinism is that human beings have the capacity to adopt a wide range of beliefs and behaviors. The central theoretical principle of the paradigm states that patterns of individual thought and behavior are molded by the influence of culture. (Of course, "patterns of thought and behavior" and "culture" are one and the same thing, but all paradigms are characterized by similar sorts of circularity. Barbara Price [1982:712–713] observes that any paradigm must argue in a circular fashion "to the extent that its task is to define certain problems as important and to direct the strategies by which such problems may be most profitably addressed.") The misnamed Sapir-Whorf "hypothesis," which holds that patterns of thought and perception are influenced by the structure of language, is an example of a particular theory produced by cultural determinism. The notion that the members of a given culture might be unable to distinguish between red and orange color chips because their language lacked terms for such a distinction would be an example of a particular testable hypothesis generated by a cultural determinist research strategy.

The concept of culture is central to the paradigm of cultural determinism, just as it is central to all anthropological paradigms. Virtually all anthropologists are cultural determinists in the sense that all anthropologists reject biological determinism. The paradigm of cultural determinism, however, does not move beyond the premise that culture determines behavior. If anthropologists wish to invoke more precise or more particular premises, they must appeal to more particular anthropological paradigms.

In the pursuit of normal science, cultural determinists seek to identify the range and diversity of human thought and behavior and to explain that range and diversity by reference to the determinative influence of culture. The relationships between culture and various facets of human experience—such as language, personality, medicine, religion, world view, and the like—make up the principal puzzles that confront cultural determinists.

Admittedly, cultural determinism and Harris's eclecticism have much in common. Like eclecticism, cultural determinism is vague and ill-defined. Its theories often are unrelated and occasionally contradictory. Moreover, the theoretical principles of cultural determinism are not sufficiently precise or elegant to provide a general framework capable of parsimoniously integrating a large number of theories. Cultural determinism is comparative and nomothetic (or attempts to be), but its various theories lack systematic and coherent integration.

Is there any real difference, then, between cultural determinism and eclecticism? I think there is, and I think there are far more cultural determinists than eclectics in contemporary anthropology. The explanations offered by cultural determinists generally can be reduced to the formula "culture determines behavior and belief"; for the most part, cultural determinists ignore the question "What determines culture?" However, ignoring that question is not the same as affirming—as Harris's eclectics purportedly do—that materialism and idealism might be equally probable explanations of "what determines culture." Rather than being strategically agnostic, most anthropologists are generally (albeit implicitly and unreflectively) committed to the strategy of cultural determinism. Eclecticism as Harris defines it—namely, the unsystematic application of commensurable paradigms to similar problems—is the exception rather than the rule among contemporary anthropologists.

By way of example, George Foster's "image of limited good" and Oscar Lewis's "culture of poverty" are both described by Harris (1979:287–314) as eclectic concepts, yet both actually are products of research pursued under the auspices of cultural determinism. Cultural materialists reject the implication that "emic and mental superstructures" such as the "image of limited good" and the "culture of poverty" cause rural and urban poverty. Foster and Lewis, however, did not imply that rural and urban poverty are "caused" by any particular world view. The task they set for themselves was to identify and describe the distinctive patterns of thought and behavior characteristic of particular subcultures, not to identify and explain the operative processes that brought those patterns of thought and behavior into being.

Cultural determinism and cultural materialism, in fact, rarely contradict one another, for the simple reason that they rarely address one another's problems. Foster and Lewis did not assert the primacy of superstructural components over infrastructural components, although, of course, neither did they admit the primacy of the infrastructure over the superstructure. Instead, they avoided the question of cultural causality altogether. The contention that the "image of limited good" and the "culture of poverty" are predictable responses to certain conditions of economic deprivation is entirely consistent with the principles of cultural materialism. Foster and Lewis neglected to explicitly address that contention, but their analyses did not preclude it. (The paradigmatic confusion surrounding the debate about the image of limited good will be discussed in detail in Chapter 15.)

Given that cultural determinism and cultural materialism are largely incommensurable, the evaluation of their relative merit cannot be based upon a direct comparison of their respective theories. That comparison instead must address the relative coherence and parsimony of the two paradigms and the relative "importance" of their respective problems. From everything that has been said to this point, it can be inferred that cultural determinism, relatively speaking, is theoretically impoverished. There is nothing especially wrong with the paradigm—its theoretical assumptions are shared by virtually every anthropological research strategy, with the exception of sociobiology—but it is not a particularly productive paradigm. The theoretical principles of cultural determinism are imprecise and unrefined.

I would suggest, then, that anthropologists would do well to abandon the paradigm of cultural determinism. Nevertheless, no paradigm, no matter how incoherent and unparsimonious its theoretical principles or how unimportant its problems, can be rejected or abandoned except in favor of some superior alternative. Paradigms can be displaced only by other paradigms. To my mind, the three most interesting candidates to replace cultural determinism are cultural materialism, structuralism, and symbolic anthropology.

These three paradigms are incommensurable because they identify different problems for investigation and specify different means of solution. As explained in Chapter 3, the evaluation of incommensurable paradigms must be based upon a consideration of each paradigm's intrinsic merit and a consideration of each paradigm's relative value. Does the paradigm address well-defined questions in a consistent and coherent fashion? Are its theories testable and falsifiable? Does the paradigm produce "true" explanations? Which paradigm addresses and solves the most "important" problems? In Chapters 10, 11, and 12, I will consider first the intrinsic merits of cultural materialism, structuralism, and symbolic anthropology in turn. After reviewing their epistemological and theoretical principles, I will then be in a position, in Chapter 13, to consider the relative value or significance of the questions addressed by each paradigm.

Suggestions for Further Reading

There are numerous works identifying and discussing the range of paradigms in anthropology, the most important and valuable of which are *The Rise of Anthropological Theory* and *Cultural Materialism,* by Marvin Harris (1968; 1979); *Main Currents in Cultural Anthropology,* edited by Naroll and Naroll (1973); *Images of Man,* by Annemarie de Waal Malefijt (1974); and *The Development of Anthropological Ideas,* by John Honigmann (1976).

See also Bohannan and Glazer (1973) and Barrett (1984).

10

The Paradigm
of Cultural Materialism

The paradigm of cultural materialism is concerned with the question of cultural causality. "The aim of cultural materialism in particular is to account for the origin, maintenance, and change of the global inventory of sociocultural differences and similarities" (Harris 1979:27). For most cultural materialists, the goals of cultural materialism and anthropology are one and the same. According to Harris (ibid.:170), the "'final aim of anthropology' . . . is the achievement of a scientific knowledge of the causes of the divergent and convergent evolutionary trajectories of sociocultural systems."

The epistemological principles of cultural materialism are explicitly scientific. As formulated by Harris (ibid.:27), cultural materialism "seeks to restrict fields of inquiry to events, entities, and relationships that are knowable by means of explicit, logico-empirical, inductive-deductive, quantifiable public procedures or 'operations' subject to replication by independent observers." Basic to the epistemological viewpoint of cultural materialism is the recognition of "the consummate importance of the difference between emic and etic knowledge" (ibid.:32). Because the study of the human experience necessarily involves the study of both thought and behavior—or the study, on the one hand, of the internal and unobservable activity of the mind and, on the other, of the external and observable activity of the body—cultural materialists conclude that there are emic and etic ways of studying thought and behavior. The result, according to Harris (ibid.:38), is the existence of four distinct ways of knowing about human social life: the emic-mental, the emic-behavioral, the etic-mental, and the etic-behavioral.

The theoretical principles of cultural materialism are founded upon four assumptions about the biopsychological nature of human beings. Harris describes those four "pan-human bio-psychological drives and predispositions" as follows:

> 1. People need to eat and will generally choose diets that offer more rather than fewer calories and proteins and other nutrients.
> 2. People cannot be totally inactive, but when confronted with a given task, they prefer to carry it out by expending less rather than more energy.
> 3. People are highly sexed and generally find reinforcing pleasure from sexual intercourse—more often from heterosexual intercourse.
> 4. People need love and affection in order to feel secure and happy, and other things being equal, they will act to increase the love and affection which others give them (ibid.:62–63).

Based upon this brief list of biopsychological constants, cultural materialists infer the existence of a universal pattern of sociocultural systems. Although frequently misrepresented as a tripartite structure, that universal pattern actually has four components (ibid.:52–54). The first of these is the *etic behavioral infrastructure*, which consists of the modes of production and reproduction or "the technology and the practices employed for expanding or limiting basic subsistence production . . . [and] for expanding, limiting, and maintaining population size." The second component of the universal pattern is the *etic behavioral structure*, which comprises the domestic and political economies or the structures responsible for "the organization of reproduction and basic production, exchange, and consumption within camps, houses, apartments, or other domestic settings . . . [and] within and between bands, villages, chiefdoms, states, and empires." The third is the *etic behavioral superstructure*, which consists of universally recurrent "productive behavior that leads to . . . recreational, sportive, and aesthetic products and services," including art, ritual, sports, and science. The fourth and final component is the *emic mental superstructure* "running roughly parallel to the etic behavioral components" and consisting of "the conscious and unconscious cognitive goals, categories, rules, plans, values, philosophies, and beliefs about behavior," including magic, religion, taboos, symbols, and ideologies.

The fundamental theoretical principle of cultural materialism is the principle of infrastructural determinism. Harris (ibid.:55–56) states the principle this way: "The etic behavioral modes of production and reproduction probabilistically determine the etic behavioral domestic and political economy, which in turn probabilistically determine the behavioral and mental emic superstructures." The determinative influence of the infrastructure stems from the fact that human beings are subject to immutable natural laws governing the acquisition of life-sustaining energy. The principle of infrastructural determinism, according to Harris, merely provides a set of strategic priorities in the search for causal factors; cultural materialists do "not deny the possibility that emic, mental, superstructural, and structural components may achieve a degree of autonomy from the etic behavioral infrastructure" (ibid.:56). Instead, cultural materialists concentrate their search for causal factors within the etic behavioral infrastructure, in the belief that, in most cases, the crucial causal factors usually will be found there.

The first apparent virtue of cultural materialism is the admirably explicit nature of its epistemological and theoretical principles. I can agree with Harris (1979:26) that "the time is ripe . . . to replace the inchoate and unconscious paradigms under whose auspices most anthropologists conduct their research with explicit descriptions of basic objectives, rules, and assumptions." Few contemporary paradigms have met that challenge as well as cultural materialism has. In addition, few other paradigms are as forthright in their response to the challenge of knowledge. The epistemological principles of cultural materialism leave no room for the possibility of epistemic relativity. The theories, predictions, and retrodictions of cultural materialism are falsifiable or aspire to be so; the knowledge gained under the auspices of cultural materialism is self-correcting to a significant degree.

A second major virtue of the paradigm lies, as claimed, in "the cogency of its substantive theories" (Harris 1979:77). The major theoretical principle of cultural materialism is parsimonious almost to a fault, yet that principle generates a broad range of specific, testable theories that are applicable to a wide variety of problems. The explanations proposed by cultural materialism are coherent and interrelated. Cultural materialists have demonstrated incontrovertibly that sociocultural systems adjust themselves in patterned and predictable ways to ecological and demographic constraints. The intellectual and moral implications of that knowledge are far-reaching.

Moreover, cultural materialism is the best paradigm yet developed by anthropologists to explain the "causes" of sociocultural phenomena. Any explanation of causality raises the problem of infinite regression. Having explained "what determines culture," cultural materialists are hard pressed to explain "what determines whatever determines culture," although the fault lies not with cultural materialists but with the intractability of causality. From a pragmatic perspective, it is sufficient for causal explanations that the causes be temporally prior to the effects they supposedly engendered and that they be different in kind from the effect produced. (Without this second criterion, there is the problem of having effects cause related effects, leaving unanswered the question of what caused the original effects. In other words, any explanation of sociocultural causality must refer to extracultural factors, and this is precisely what cultural materialism does by pointing to the determinative influence of energetic and other material constraints.) Cultural materialist explanations of cultural causality are considerably more satisfying than those that assert that culture is determined by tradition.

Note, however, that cultural materialism is not capable of explaining the causes of all sociocultural phenomena, as cultural materialists recognize. Cultural materialism cannot explain many of the particularities of emic mental superstructures, such as, for example, "the rule that boy babies get blue blankets and girl babies get pink blankets" (Harris 1982:142). Nor are there any infrastructural determinants of the principal features of the phonemic and grammatical structures of particular languages (Harris 1979:55). In addition, cultural materialism is concerned primarily with the general question of cultural causality (that is, which sociocultural system component is determinative) and not the particular question of dynamic processes (for example, the "innovative" processes identified by Barnett [1953]). Instead, cultural materialism offers causal explanations for those sociocultural phenomena that either benefit or detract from the productive and reproductive efforts of particular sociocultural systems. In effect, the principle of infrastructural determinism is only capable of accounting for those components of sociocultural systems that are affected by infrastructural determinants. That circularity is hardly a criticism of the paradigm, however. The kinds of answers obtained depend upon the kinds of questions asked. Granted, there are many interesting and important questions about the human experience that are not addressed by cultural materialism. What is remarkable, nevertheless, is how well (that is, how parsimoniously, coherently, and cogently) cultural materialism answers the questions it does address.

Ironically (and unfortunately), most critiques of cultural materialism fault the paradigm for failing to address questions it was not designed to address. The most common error among critics of cultural materialism is to equate the principle of infrastructural determinism with a form of economic reductionism. It is an error made by those who insist upon the obvious truth that human beings are motivated by irrational, emotional urges as well as by rational assessments of practical costs and benefits. According to these critics, cultural materialism reduces individual human beings to automatons and overlooks the manifest complexity of individual behavior.

Such criticisms are inappropriate for the simple reason that cultural materialism has nothing to do with individual behavior. The paradigm is designed instead to account for the existence of cultural systems of behavior; as Harris (1984:649) says, "Cultural materialism does not predict the behavior of individuals; it predicts (or retrodicts) the behavior of aggregates of individuals."

Harris made that comment in response to an article by Drew Westen entitled "Cultural Materialism: Food for Thought or Bum Steer?" Westen (1984:645) claims that cultural materialism is "irremediably flawed," and he says "it is time we put to rest the misbegotten hope that we will ever reduce meaning to mechanism and begin to work toward an understanding of that peculiar species that thrives on symbols as well as proteins."

Westen makes the fundamental error of failing to distinguish between individual behavior and cultural systems of behavior: "Cultural materialism rests on an untenable psychology. . . . The problem is that such analysis [involving appeal to the principle of infrastructural determinism] is emic and mental, not infrastructural and behavioral, and therefore the ultimate causes of behavior and culture must be superstructural" (Westen 1984:643).

Jeffrey Ehrenreich (1984:648) correctly points out the faults in Westen's argument: "A major problem with Westen's analysis is that he would have us believe that cultural materialism is a view of a social or individual psychology rather than an approach to and perspective on the origins and causes of macro-patterns of cultural development. . . . At no time does the strategy of cultural materialism attempt to explain the nuances of all individual behavior or cognition."

Westen makes another mistake in his assessment of cultural materialism, a mistake that is perhaps the second most common error among the paradigm's detractors—namely, the logical mistake of assuming that the origins of science have something somehow to do with the validity of the scientific approach: "If science is superstructural, then a particular science is to be explained in terms of the infrastructure that gave birth to it, in this case American capitalism. To be consistent, then, Harris must be willing to accept . . . [the] criticism that his explanation of sociocultural phenomena in terms of rational cost benefit analysis is a reflection of an ethnocentric bourgeois view" (Westen 1984:642).

The logical errors of this argument have been discussed already, but to recapitulate briefly, in Ehrenreich's (1984:647) terms, "Science is a *technique* for perceiving, deciphering, and understanding reality—*any* [empirical] *reality"* (emphasis in original). It does not matter that the technique of science is the product of a bourgeois culture; to suggest that it does matter is simply prejudice. What matters is whether science does or does not satisfy the requirements of epistemological responsibility. That is an exclusively epistemological question, and an exclusively epistemological answer must be given. (I have given my answer in Chapter 2.)

What matters with respect to cultural materialism is how well the paradigm fulfills its own promise, and here we can find legitimate areas for criticism. For example, although no contemporary paradigm makes as rigorous an epistemological distinction between emic and etic types of knowledge as cultural materialism does, that distinction is not completely unambiguous. Harris (1979:38) argues that "if the terms 'emic' and 'etic' are not redundant with respect to the terms 'mental' and 'behavioral,' there should be four objective operationally definable domains in the sociocultural field of inquiry." In fact, however, the terms *emic* and *etic* are operationally redundant with respect to the terms *mental* and *behavioral*. The four "domains of inquiry" include two operationally unrealizable domains, namely, the emic-behavioral and the etic-mental.

Analyses of the emics of behavior necessarily consider the cognitive context of behavior. As those analyses are concerned with the way in which behavior is perceived and interpreted, they are concerned with the emics of mental life. Similarly, analyses of the etics of thought necessarily involve inferences from the observations of behavior and are concerned accordingly with the etics of behavior. The issue, after all, is epistemology. More specifically, the issue here is operationalism, or the method of inquiry. The emics of behavior can be known only through the emics of thought, while the etics of thought can be known only through the etics of behavior.

In certain respects, this conclusion may seem counterintuitive. Given the fact that human experience comprises two distinct realms, thought and behavior, and the fact that two distinct forms of cultural analysis are possible, the emic and the etic, it would seem, on the surface, to be eminently reasonable to assume via a simple mathematical permutation that four distinct domains of inquiry exist. But consider, for example, the epistemological consequences of investigations conducted in the etic-mental domain. The "thought" that is etically described either is or is not in the minds of the people for whom the description is offered. If that thought is absent, then it is merely an etic construct inferred from behavior and as such does not merit the appellation "mental." If that thought is present, then there should be some means of eliciting it through the exploration of the emic-mental domain.

One way around this difficulty, of course, is to claim that the thought is present but unelicitable because it is unconscious. That claim, however, rests upon an assumption that is neither empirically testable nor logically falsifiable. If the informant never "admits" to having the thought, the only way to demonstrate its existence is by reference to its behavioral manifestation—but that is nothing more than the etics of behavior. If the informant does "admit" to having the thought, then his or her admission thus belongs to the emic-mental domain.

I want to be certain that the thrust of my criticism of cultural materialism's epistemological principles is clear. Statements describing the emics of behavior are different in form and content from statements describing the emics of mental life. In the same way, analyses of the etics of thought are couched in terms that are foreign to analyses of the etics of behavior. The four distinct "domains of inquiry" do exist as four distinct domains of description and analysis. But they are not distinct operational domains of inquiry. Although different questions are posed to informants in the effort to obtain answers that may be classed, alternately, as the emics of behavior or the emics of thought, in both cases the method for verifying knowledge is the same, namely, elicitation of the informant's world view. Etic knowledge, on the other hand, can be validated only by the observation of behavior, whether it is etic knowledge of thought or behavior that is sought. What is going on in the mind of an informant can be known only by the informant's report. Some psychics claim to be able to perceive directly other people's states of mind, but those claims have not been sufficiently substantiated. Operationally speaking, the emics of behavior and the etics of thought do not exist. (Indeed, the "emic-behavioral" and the "etic-mental" components are properly absent from the universal pattern described by cultural materialists.)

Cultural materialism has been criticized for being overly "deterministic," for advocating "single factor" causality, and for being "antihuman." None of these criticisms is warranted. Cultural materialism hardly can be faulted for failing to contribute to exclusively "humanistic" or "aesthetic" analyses of the human experience because cultural materialism is manifestly unconcerned with such analyses. When cultural materialism is charged with omitting the "human" element from its description of sociocultural systems, those charges usually are vague and devoid of propositional meaning. Most such charges are merely emotive reaffirmations of the value of research pursued under nonmaterialist paradigms, and, as such, hardly can be considered substantive critiques of cultural materialism. There is, however, one meaningful sense in which cultural materialism neglects the "human" element. To discover that sense, we have to look not at cultural materialism's incommensurable competitors, but at the consistency and coherency of cultural materialism's theoretical assumptions.

The universal pattern postulated by cultural materialism is based upon four universal human characteristics: the need for nutrition, the preference for the least possible expenditure of energy, the motivation for sexual intercourse, and the desire for sociability and affect. As Harris (1979:63) admits, exceptions to each of these panhuman drives and predispositions can be readily adduced. Nevertheless, each of these characteristics is unquestionably true about the great majority of human beings throughout time and space. The most problematic assumption is the premise of least effort, but that too seems well established cross-culturally, especially if the assumption is generally restricted to efforts to obtain life-sustaining energy. As Harris also observes, the valued parsimony of cultural materialism's theoretical principles is due in part to the brevity of the paradigm's list of biopsychological traits.

Harris offers another justification for the list's brevity, however, which poses some difficulties. The validity and generality of those four assumptions, he argues, are "guaranteed by the existence of similar biopsychological predispositions among most members of the primate order" (Harris 1979:63). Restricting the list to four more or less panprimate predispositions ensures that we will not be tempted to reduce "every recurrent cultural trait to the status of a biological given" (ibid.). The question that then presents itself, however, is why the human species should have developed sociocultural systems at all. If most primates share these same characteristics, why do not most primates have sociocultural systems as well? What is it that makes the human species different?

In short, cultural materialism's list of biopsychological universals omits the one universal predisposition that is quintessentially human, namely the fact that human beings are meaning-seeking, symbol-using animals. Given cultural materialism's four biopsychological assumptions, the universal existence of etic behavioral modes of production and reproduction and the ubiquitous occurrence of etic behavioral domestic and political economies are entirely understandable and predictable. But why should all sociocultural systems include an etic behavioral superstructure? Even more to the point, why should all sociocultural systems have an emic mental superstructure? Nothing in the list of universal human predispositions suggested by cultural materialism explains the reliable recurrence of superstructures.

Eric Gans raises this same issue in his critique of cultural materialism. He argues that "man is not distinguished from the animals by his propensity to economic activity but by his use of representation" (Gans 1985:88), and he observes that Harris "devotes much of his energy to explaining representations away, but not to explaining either why they exist in the first place or why they so fascinate him and his readers" (ibid.:89).

I would suggest, then, that cultural materialism could be improved by adding a single assumption about the biopsychological characteristics of the human species, namely, that people will assign meanings to their activities and experiences and will invest considerable intellectual and emotional currency in the development, expression, and preservation of those meanings.

It should be noted that the significance of this universal human predisposition is far from entirely lost on cultural materialists. Cultural materialism insists upon the importance of the emic/etic distinction precisely because of the universal existence of elicitable meanings. Indeed, Harris (1979:52) affirms that the universal recurrence of the etic behavioral superstructure is based upon "the prominence of human speech acts and the importance of symbolic processes for the human psyche." Elsewhere (in the third edition of his textbook *Culture, People, Nature*), he writes that the most important part of human nature is the symbolic capacity for creative activity. That assumption, however, is too fundamental and too critical to be omitted from any list of essential human traits. Cultural materialism fails to stress that assumption because cultural materialism is largely unconcerned with discovering and explaining the nature of symbolic processes per se (although cultural materialists do recognize that "communication . . . serves a vital instrumental role in coordinating infrastructural, structural, and superstructural activities" [Harris 1979:54]). In the interests of consistency and coherency, however, cultural materialism would do well to incorporate that assumption at its core. Of course, that additional premise opens up entirely new fields of investigation. Structuralism and symbolic anthropology, as we shall see, are concerned primarily with exploring the implications of the fact that human beings are preeminently meaning-seeking animals.

One final criticism that has been made of cultural materialism deserves consideration, and that is Magnarella's (1982) observation that there is an apparent discrepancy between the paradigm's stated logic and its logic in use, particularly with respect to cultural materialism's theoretical principles and their application in empirical research. In the stated logic of cultural materialism, the principle of infrastructural determinism is carefully qualified. Harris (1979:56) claims that

> cultural materialists give highest priority to the effort to formulate and test theories in which infrastructural variables are the primary causal factors . . . [while] theories that bestow causal primacy upon the mental and emic superstructure are to be formulated and tested only as an ultimate

recourse when no testable etic behavioral theories can be formulated or when all that have been formulated have been decisively discredited.

As Magnarella notes, cultural materialism's logic in use is a different matter because research pursued under the auspices of cultural materialism rarely if ever fails to identify infrastructural determinants. If cultural materialists can always discover infrastructural determinants, then how can cultural materialism claim to be falsifiable? Do infrastructural determinants "really" exist, or are they merely "theoretical" constructs of the paradigm? A related problem (which Magnarella also notes) is the difficulty involved in identifying which infrastructural variable is most determinative in any given instance. How do we choose between two alternative materialist explanations, when, for example, one implicates an aspect of the mode of production and the other implicates an aspect of the mode of reproduction as being causally determinative?

Neither of these problems is fatal for cultural materialism, however. In the first place, although the theoretical principle of infrastructural determinism is not itself falsifiable, the particular theories to which that theoretical principle gives rise are falsifiable. As Harris (1982:145) notes in his reply to Magnarella, the predictions made by cultural materialists— such as "the prediction that the declining U.S. fertility rate is not a temporary aberration"—are eminently falsifiable. Moreover, cases of superstructural determinism do exist and are recognized by cultural materialists (Harris mentions the Iranian Islamic and Chinese cultural revolutions), although cultural materialists predict that such changes will usually not persist if they are at odds with infrastructural conditions. That claim, too, is falsifiable. It could be falsified simply by adducing a substantial (that is, more than unusual) number of cases in which superstructural determinism has inspired long-term changes in the face of infrastructural opposition. (Cultural materialists, of course, can point to a large number of cases in which infrastructural determinism has inspired long-term changes despite superstructural opposition. The shift from a production economy to a service economy in the United States after World War II, for example, radically altered the sexual composition of the labor force, which in turn brought about the collapse of traditional sexual morality despite fierce superstructural opposition [Harris 1981b].)

In the second place, the problem of identifying critical infrastructural determinants is an empirical problem, not a logical one. Competing cultural materialist theories or explanations obviously would be commensurable; evaluating the relative efficacy of competing materialist claims therefore would be a logically simple, even if empirically difficult, task. The failure to accomplish that task would invalidate the work of the individual cultural materialist, not the paradigm itself. One of the challenges of scientific theory is to apply the theory properly (that is, rigorously, systematically, consistently, and accurately).

Magnarella is correct in pointing out, however, that the precise procedures and techniques of research under the auspices of cultural materialism have not yet been specified. The paradigm should offer guidance as to how various probabilities of causality are to be identified, weighed, and evaluated. The failure to do so, again, hardly invalidates cultural materialism—it simply means that the paradigm needs refinement.

Suggestions for Further Reading

Marvin Harris (1968) first discusses the paradigm of cultural materialism in *The Rise of Anthropological Theory*; the most complete articulation and defense of the research strategy can be found in *Cultural Materialism* (Harris 1979).

11

The Paradigm
of Structuralism

The paradigm of structuralism is concerned ultimately with the structure of the human mind—not the neurological structure of the brain, but the logical structure of human thought processes. Structuralism seeks to uncover the hidden nature of thought and to show how panhuman thought processes are manifested in culturally diverse situations. According to Claude Levi-Strauss (1963:274), structuralism's founder and chief advocate, "the structural method consists in perceiving invariant forms within different contexts." Following a linguistic analogy, structuralism concerns itself with the "deep structure" underlying cultural phenomena. Structuralists are much less concerned with the apparent reality of surface features than they are with the fundamental reality of submerged features. "When we consider some system of belief . . . or some form of social organization . . . the question we ask is 'What does it all mean?' To answer it, we attempt to *translate* into our language rules originally conceived in another language" (Levi-Strauss 1976:10). Elsewhere, Levi-Strauss characterizes his structuralist endeavors in these terms: "I have always aimed at drawing up an inventory of mental patterns, to reduce apparently arbitrary data to some kind of order, and to attain a level at which a kind of necessity becomes apparent, underlying the illusions of liberty" (1969b:10).

The central problem addressed by the paradigm of structuralism, as Leach (1970:36) perceptively notes, is simply this: What is Man? To answer that question, structuralists point to the invariant face of human thought lying behind the many masks of culture. This "problem of invariance," writes Levi-Strauss (1976:24), is the problem of "the universality of human nature." Structuralists affirm implicitly that human beings are quintessentially meaning-seeking animals. Structuralism aims to discover the universal cognitive processes by which human beings assign meaning to and derive meaning from their experiences. Harris (1979:166) is correct in observing that "structuralism is a set of principles for studying the mental superstructure."

The specific goal of structuralism, according to Levi-Strauss (1969b:1), is "to prove that there is a kind of logic in tangible qualities, and to demonstrate the operation of that logic and reveal its laws." Like cultural materialists, structuralists regard the goals of anthropology as essentially congruent with the aims of their paradigm. Thus Levi-Strauss (1976:9–10) conceives anthropology to be "the *bona fide* occupant of that domain of semiology which linguistics has not already claimed for its own." "The final aim of anthropology," he asserts on another occasion, "is to contribute to a better knowledge of objectified thought and its mechanisms" (Levi-Strauss 1969b:13). So far, the realms of "objectified thought" analyzed by structuralists have included such diverse phenomena as kinship, totemism, mythology, cuisine, table manners, and stoplights.

The epistemological principles of structuralism derive from the paradigm's ontological assumptions. The subject matter of structuralism is an unseen, hidden reality that lies behind the empirical world. As such, structuralists can hardly restrict themselves to measurable, quantifiable, "objective" epistemological procedures, as do cultural materialists. Instead, structural analysis depends upon the intuitive imagination of the analyst. There is method to the structuralist's madness (Levi-Strauss 1963), but it is not a method that is easily and exactly replicated. For Levi-Strauss (ibid.:23), the anthropologist's "goal is to grasp, beyond the conscious and always shifting images which men hold, the complete range of unconscious possibilities." That range, of course, is limited, and the theoretical principles of structuralism are intended to define its scope and properties. But if the anthropologist "applies his [or her] analysis primarily to the unconscious elements of social life" (ibid.), then anthropological analysis is fundamentally concerned with the etics of thought. Given that knowledge of the "etic mental" domain can be obtained only by inference, structuralists derive those inferences from their analyses of emic mental domains.

The theoretical principles of structuralism attempt to account for the modes of human thought. Levi-Strauss (1963:21) expresses the paradigm's raison d'être in this fashion: "If . . . the unconscious activity of the mind consists in imposing forms upon content, and if these forms are fundamentally the same for all minds . . . it is necessary and sufficient to grasp the unconscious structure underlying each institution and each custom, in order to obtain a principle of interpretation valid for other institutions and other customs." The structuralist "principle of interpretation" holds that an unconscious dialectic of binary oppositions underlies all "objectified thoughts." This dichotomous pattern of thought is presumed to be a universal human characteristic, as is the search for third elements that mediate the oppositions. Structuralists claim to have demonstrated that people cross-culturally are preoccupied with the same binary oppositions, the principal one of which is the opposition between "culture" and "nature." According to the structuralist argument, the maintenance of human identity is accomplished by the maintenance of the culture/nature dichotomy. Other common oppositions include self and other, male and female, life and death, and sacred and profane.

Structuralism is not explicitly "idealist" in that it maintains that structures of thought determine culture. Instead, as Malefijt (1974:325) notes, structuralists recognize that patterns of thought "operate within a cultural context." For Levi-Strauss, culture is a product not of the mind but of the interaction that goes on between the mind and human activity (Murphy 1980:185; Rossi 1974:98). Structuralists are aware that there are particular historical, economic, and environmental determinants of particular cultural forms but are not interested in identifying or analyzing those determinative factors. Rather, structuralists are interested in identifying and analyzing the common unconscious structures that underlie diverse cultural forms. For structuralists, the more things change, the more they stay the same. (Of course, the same is true in one sense for cultural materialists. Amid the temporal and spatial diversity of cultural forms stands the invariant fact that sociocultural systems systematically adjust themselves to material constraints.) But, for structuralists, change is not the issue.

A notable deficiency of structuralism, in sharp contrast to cultural materialism, is the imprecision of its epistemological and theoretical principles. True, Levi-Strauss does offer general guidelines for the conduct of structural analysis. He declares, for example, that the "principles which serve as a basis for any kind of structural analysis [are] economy of explanation, unity of solution, and [the] ability to reconstruct the whole from a fragment" (1963:211). But how is structural analysis to be arrived at in the first place? Is there any guarantee that independent structuralists will adduce the same structural explanation in any given instance? Levi-Strauss does not offer satisfactory answers to these questions. In the final analysis, the "correct" or "true" structural analysis is the one that appeals most forcefully, in some intuitive way, to the intellect and imagination. As Werner (1973:295) has noted, the work of Levi-Strauss contains few summaries of either theory or method. Although structuralism is a paradigm designed to investigate the structure of the human mind, it is a paradigm that has produced remarkably few theories about human thought processes. As Malefijt (1974:331) observes, "So far, he [Levi-Strauss] does not say much more about the human mind than that it *is* structured, and that its tendency is to think in binary patterns" (emphasis in original).

I have said that structuralism is avowedly unconcerned with change, but I also have noted that structuralism is concerned primarily with explaining the nature of the mental superstructure. It is an unavoidable fact that change is a salient characteristic of the mental superstructure. All mental superstructures are changing all the time, and that presents a problem for structuralism. Granted, structuralism is not concerned with explaining the causes of superstructural change, and to fault the paradigm for its failure to do so would be to beg the materialist question. Nevertheless, it is difficult to be completely satisfied by structuralist explanations when those explanations fail utterly to account for an obvious feature of the domain to which they are applied. Structuralists assume perpetual "surface" change to be a given, and they are content to demonstrate that the same fundamental patterns of thought underlie all such changes. But why is it that human beings show so little loyalty to particular "objectified thoughts" that are "good to think"? If it is satisfying to arrange particular thoughts in a dichotomous pattern, why are the satisfactions derived from those particular arrangements so ephemeral? Is it that human beings simply are inclined to assign meaning in a dichotomous pattern and are wholly unconcerned with the particular content of the meaning assigned? If so, why? The failure to address these questions is another deficiency of the structuralist paradigm.

In addition, there is a significant discrepancy between structuralism's stated logic and its logic in use. Despite the fact that structuralists recognize that patterns of thought "operate within a particular context" and that there are extracultural determinants of cultural forms, and despite Levi-Strauss's stated belief in the "undoubted primacy of the infrastructure," many particular structuralist arguments closely resemble briefs for superstructural determinism. In *The Savage Mind*, for example, Levi-Strauss surveys the extensive floral and faunal knowledge held by primitives around the world and suggests that "one may readily conclude that animals and plants are not known as the result of their usefulness; they are deemed to be useful or interesting because they are first of all known" (1966:9). It might be argued in this instance that the discrepancy between structuralism's stated logic and its logic in use is more apparent than real. After all, not all superstructural components have infrastructural determinants; many are infrastructurally neutral. As Levi-Strauss has argued in another context, "To say that a society functions is a truism; to say that everything in a society functions is an absurdity" (1963:13). Levi-Strauss simply may be suggesting that the extent and complexity of floral and faunal knowledge in various cultures are due in part to the human predilection to create worlds of meaning. But there are other instances in which Levi-Strauss's superstructural determinism is more blatant.

The status of the coyote in native American mythology is an example of one such puzzle. Levi-Strauss poses the problem in this way: "Why is it that throughout North America his [the trickster's] role is assigned practically everywhere to either coyote or raven?" (1963:224). Thus phrased, the question is one of cultural causality. What accounts for this particular cross-cultural similarity? Levi-Strauss claims that the answer lies in the fact that "mythical thought always progresses from the awareness of oppositions toward their resolution" (ibid.). The coyote is a trickster because, as a carrion-eater, it is an anomalous animal, mediating between plant-eating animals and beasts of prey. Plant-eating animals and beasts of prey are associated, respectively, with agriculture and hunting. Agriculture and hunting, in turn, suggest the opposition between life and death. Hence the coyote is anomalous cross-culturally because all cultures recognize the opposition between life and death.

In this case, Levi-Strauss seems to be saying that universal dichotomous patterns of thought have determined the recurrence of a particular cultural feature. Harris (1979:200–201) objects that Levi-Strauss's account is far too arcane. Harris suggests instead a much more mundane explanation: The coyote enjoys the status of a trickster because it is an intelligent, opportunistic animal. Of course, the problem here may be merely one of expository style. Perhaps what Levi-Strauss is really saying is that all cultures construct sets of binary oppositions and their mediators after the fact—that is, having recognized a wily animal, they construct an emic typology that will render that animal anomalous. ("Herbivore" and "carnivore," after all, are categories developed by human beings, not inalienable aspects of the "real" world.)

To escape the charge of superstructural determinism, structuralists often have to resort to just such fancy footwork. The failure to rule out arguments that appeal to superstructural determinism is yet another deficiency of the paradigm. In its stated logic, however—and often in its logic in use—structuralism does not address questions of cultural causality. In order to evaluate the paradigm, therefore, it is necessary to critique structuralism's occasional references to superstructural determinism, but it is not sufficient to do so.

The most significant and fundamental criticism that has been made of structuralism is that structural analyses simply are not true. One of the most frequently quoted of all structuralist statements is Levi-Strauss's (1963:279) declaration that "the term 'social structure' has nothing to do with empirical reality but with models which are built up after it." As Malefijt (1974:331) observes, the implication that "structuralism seems to have no relevance to the empirical world" is especially disturbing to a great many anthropologists. Are the unconscious structures identified by structural analysis really there at all? Harris (1979:167) suggests that "there is a distinct possibility that structuralist structures exist only in the imaginations of the structuralists themselves." Jenkins (1979) argues that structural analyses are inherently unreal and that structuralism is hopelessly unscientific. Diamond (1974:325) claims that the work of Levi-Strauss "represents a triumph of inauthenticity." Werner (1973:295–299) insists that structuralism is unsystematic; that structural analysis fails to account for all of the constituent elements within its domain of inquiry; and that structuralist claims are neither testable nor falsifiable. These are all serious charges, which, if substantiated, might be expected to entail the demise of structuralism as a legitimate paradigm. It is important therefore to understand the import of Levi-Strauss's startling response to these attacks.

Rather than insist that structural analyses are falsifiable, Levi-Strauss claims instead that structuralism is not to be faulted for failing to produce falsifiable propositions: "The most fashionable objection to structural anthropology is that its hypotheses cannot be 'falsified.' Yet, this criterion can only be applied to fully established sciences. Anthropology has not yet attained this stage" (1976:viii). That is a very strange claim to make, for there are, unarguably, a great many falsifiable propositions that have come out of anthropology. Levi-Strauss is able to make that claim, however, because he has a fairly peculiar sense of what "anthropology" is all about.

> It may be said that the [structural analysis presented here] . . . takes ethnographic research in the direction of psychology, logic, and philosophy, where it has no right to venture. Am I not helping to deflect ethnography from its real task, which should be the study of native communities and the examination, from the social, political, and economic points of view, of problems posed by the relations among individuals and groups within a given community? Such misgivings . . . seem to me to arise from a total misunderstanding of what I am trying to do (1969b:9).

But what then is Levi-Strauss trying to do? If his claims are not verifiable, how is it that they promise to increase our understanding of the world? What constitutes a valid explanation in structuralist terms? Levi-Strauss offers this answer:

> For [structural analysis] to be worthwhile, it is not necessary in my view that it should be assumed to embody the truth for years to come and with regard to the tiniest detail. I shall be satisfied if it is credited with the modest achievement of having left a difficult problem in a rather less unsatisfactory state than it was before. Nor must we forget that in science there are no final truths. The scientific mind does not so much provide the right answers as ask the right questions (1969b:7).

In other words, empirical criticisms of structural analyses carry little if any weight. Structural analyses are to be evaluated according to other criteria (including economy of explanation, coherency, and comprehensiveness) and can be supplanted only by other structural interpretations. "Instead of *proving* anything about cultural phenomena," says Ino Rossi, "the structuralist is concerned with *understanding* them" (Rossi 1974:93; emphasis added). Scholte (1973:687) argues that "by transcending the phenomenally given while still retaining a concrete basis, [structural] anthropology can aspire to become a truly creative and scientific enterprise." But empiricists find it extremely frustrating to be told that their demonstrations of the unreality of structural analyses are irrelevant. Edmund Leach's structural interpretation of stoplights, for example, is, according to the standards by which structuralists determine explanatory validity, capable of surviving the most abrupt and unsettling confrontation with empirical reality.

Leach (1970:21–25) explains that the colors red and green have been selected as traffic light indicators for "stop" and "go" because red and green occur at opposite ends of the color spectrum. Yellow signifies caution because yellow, occurring in the middle of the color spectrum, mediates between red and green. Like many structuralist explanations, this one has the virtue of being clever. But, at least according to Frederick Gamst (1980), it lacks the virtue of being correct. In a historical critique of Leach's argument, Gamst demonstrates that the selection of red and green as stoplight indicators followed a period of experimentation in which several different colors (including red, green, blue, orange, and white) were used in various combinations and contexts to embody various meanings. The final red-yellow-green product, according to Gamst, "is the result of numerous reactions to practical considerations of interrelated material elements" (1980:382).

By structuralist standards, it does not matter that the people who developed traffic lights failed to have a red-green opposition in mind. Empirical attacks like the one launched by Gamst make little impression upon structuralists, for Levi-Strauss has already anticipated and dismissed all such criticisms:

> Let me say again that all the solutions put forward are not presented as being of equal value, since I myself have made a point of emphasizing the uncertainty of some of them; however, it would be hypocritical not to carry my thought to its logical conclusion. I therefore say in advance to possible critics: what does this matter? For if the final aim of anthropology is to contribute to a better knowledge of objectified thought and its mechanisms, it is in the last resort immaterial whether in this book the thought processes of the South American Indians take shape through the medium of my thoughts, or whether mine take shape through the medium of theirs. What matters is that the human mind, regardless of the identity of those who happen to be giving it expression, should display an increasingly intelligible structure as a result of the doubly reflexive thought movement of two thought processes acting one upon the other, either of which can in turn provide the spark or tinder whose conjunction will shed light on both (1969b:13).

It does not matter that the particular structural analysis advanced may be slightly off the mark, for the mere fact that a structural analysis could be performed at all demonstrates that binary thought processes are at work. Having demonstrated that fact, structuralists have reached the goal they set out to attain. Or so, apparently, runs Levi-Strauss's argument. He maintains that "structuralism uncovers a unity and a coherence within things which could not be revealed by a simple description of the facts" (Levi-Strauss 1976:ix). For structuralists, as Honigmann (1976:322) notes, "soundness [of explanation] means logical, not empirical, validity." If a given structuralist interpretation appeals forcefully to the mind and it is not supplanted by other more appealing structuralist interpretations, then it is sound. Structuralist claims to validity might be better substantiated if structuralists could persuade their informants to admit that they, too, found structural interpretations appealing and compelling. If South American Indians, for example, would explain that the particular binary oppositions described by the structural analyst were not the ones they had in mind but that they derived considerable cognitive satisfaction from contemplating the structuralist's account, we might be more inclined to believe that dichotomous patterns of thought are truly and demonstrably universal. Of course, such an exercise hardly would constitute a falsifiable test of structuralism because it would not necessarily demonstrate anything beyond the persuasiveness of the structural analyst. The inescapable conclusion is that structuralism is neither falsifiable nor scientific.

Are structural explanations in any way satisfying? The answer, as Honigmann (ibid.:329) observes, "depends partly on the kind of understanding being sought." Levi-Strauss is interested only in the kind of understanding that structural analysis yields. The understanding gained from other paradigms, in his view, cannot invalidate structuralist knowledge: "In the human sciences . . . a hypothesis only possesses a relative value, granted if it succeeds in accounting for more facts than those hypotheses it replaces; that is, until such times as another one makes a new step *in the same direction*" (Levi-Strauss 1976:ix; emphasis added). Elvin Hatch (1973:336–337) draws a distinction between interpretive or meaningful forms of explanation and "scientific" explanations. He observes that scientific explanations account for a particular event or entity by reference to some general covering law, while interpretive explanations attempt to make a phenomenon intelligible by setting that phenomenon within some meaningful context. Hatch does not address the question of whether interpretive explanations also might appeal to general covering laws and thereby might be scientific. The distinction he is making is actually between inductive-statistical explanations and deductive-nomological explanations. As discussed in Chapter 2, it is possible for both forms of explanation to be scientific. Nevertheless, structuralist explanations are "interpretive" explanations in the sense that Hatch intends—that is, structuralist explanations are unscientific. Structuralist interpretations are not satisfying if the standards for satisfactory explanations include the ability to make reliable empirical predictions, but structuralists would have their interpretations judged by different standards.

Judged by scientific standards—including the criterion of falsifiability—the paradigm of structuralism has little to offer to the systematic study of human thought and behavior. Yet I would be reluctant to say that structuralism is devoid of any merit whatsoever. The scientific enterprise is an excellent and indispensable source of insight about the human condition, but it is not the only one. (Among the others I have in mind are philosophy and literature.) Structuralism, in fact, has enjoyed a wide influence outside anthropology (see Kurzweil 1980). Leach (1970:117–118) remarks that "the genuinely valuable part of Levi-Strauss' contribution . . . [is] the truly poetic range of associations which he brings to bear in the course of his analysis." Leach observes as well that structuralism reminds us that "such practical economic matters as hunting and agriculture are inextricably entangled with attitudes towards cosmology, sanctity, food, women, life and death," and so on (ibid.:119). Structural analysis demonstrates the richness and complexity of symbolic realms. That point is of value to the scientific study of the human experience.

There may be others that are as well. Structuralism offers a useful tool for the classification and comparison of myths. In addition, structuralism has the virtue of addressing questions that are otherwise unaddressed in scientific inquiry. Why is it, for example, that rites of passage have the same tripartite structure cross-culturally? Structuralism at least makes intelligible the fact that the opposing stages of separation and incorporation are invariably mediated by a third stage of transition. Why is it that the incest taboo is found in all cultures? Edward Tylor and Leslie White have explained the taboo's functional cause, but Levi-Strauss offers an explanation of why that one particular device (the incest taboo) should have been chosen to fulfill the particular functions that it does fulfill (including intergroup alliance). (The incest taboo, according to Levi-Strauss, is the means by which humans distinguish themselves from the rest of nature.) In the absence of alternative explanations, the structuralist account at least partially releases the tension that provoked the question.

In the end, however, all structuralist accounts suffer from a crisis of confidence. No matter how clever or appealing they may be, they fail to offer the conviction of sufficient certainty. Despite its attractions, structuralism does not constitute a scientifically responsible form of inquiry. Ultimately, all structural explanations are based upon an intuitive epistemological foundation. Hence knowledge obtained by structuralism is not self-correcting, and it is subject to too few external sources of verification. These are problems, however, that the paradigm of symbolic anthropology attempts to solve.

Suggestions for Further Reading

The clearest and most comprehensive articulations of the paradigm of structuralism can be found in *Structural Anthropology, Volumes 1 and 2* by Claude Levi-Strauss (1963; 1976). Leach (1970), Geertz (1973), Naroll and Naroll (1973), Malefijt (1974), Harris (1979), Murphy (1980), and Barrett (1984) all offer valuable summations and critiques of structuralism.

12

The Paradigm of Symbolic Anthropology

The paradigm of symbolic anthropology is concerned essentially with the significance of meaning for human life. Symbolic anthropology is predicated upon the notion that human beings are first and foremost meaning-seeking, symbol-using animals. Broadly speaking, symbolic anthropologists address two fundamental questions: First, what is the significance of meaning for human identity, and second, what is the significance of meaning for the operation of human social systems? (In this context, the term *meaning* refers to shared patterns of interpretation and perspective embodied in symbols, by means of which people develop and communicate their knowledge about and attitudes toward life.) Scholte (1984b:541) summarizes the approach of symbolic anthropology in these terms: "[The paradigm] is motivated by a central issue: the problem of the concrete universal. . . . [The paradigm attempts], as it were, to tease the universal out of the specific without reducing the latter to a mere illustration of the former."

Each of the paradigm's two fundamental questions has both emic and etic dimensions. As we shall see, symbolic anthropology has devoted most of its attention to the emic aspects of human identity and symbolic process. The etic variety of that second question is also addressed, although somewhat less deliberately and with different emphasis, by other paradigms, including cultural materialism.

Symbolic anthropology, according to a major text that helped popularize the paradigm's name, "is the study of the basic terms with which we view ourselves as people and as members of society, and of how these basic terms are used by people to build for themselves a mode of life" (Dolgin, Kemnitzer, and Schneider 1977:3). By "building a mode of life," symbolic anthropologists do not intend to describe the ways in which people develop modes of production and reproduction, nor are they implying that people construct domestic and political economies out of a desire to impose meaning upon their experiences. Instead, symbolic anthropologists are referring to the perceptual context of experience—to the ways in which people build their cognitive orientations to life, or to the means by which people, as social animals, acquire knowledge and values about themselves and their world. "In the last analysis, then as in the first," writes Clifford Geertz (1983:16), the principal architect of symbolic anthropology, "the interpretative study of culture represents an attempt to come to terms with the diversity of the ways human beings construct their lives in the act of leading them."

Symbolic anthropologists place a pronounced emphasis upon the collection of emic data for its own sake. According to Dolgin, Kemnitzer, and Schneider (1977:34), "Fundamental to the study of symbolic anthropology is the concern with how people formulate their reality." Comparing emic and etic "realities" is not the mission of symbolic anthropology. "Our concern is not with whether or not the views a people hold are accurate in any 'scientific' sense of the term. . . . In social action, that which is thought to be real is treated as real" (ibid.:5). In *The Interpretation of Cultures*, one of the seminal works of symbolic anthropology, Clifford Geertz (1973:30) says that "the essential vocation of interpretive [that is, symbolic] anthropology is not to answer our deepest questions, but to make available to us answers that others . . . have given, and thus to include them in the consultable record of what man has said." In *Local Knowledge*, Geertz (1983:5) expands on that theme: "My own work . . . represents an effort . . . to understand how it is we understand understandings not our own."

The principal aim of symbolic anthropology is to elicit answers about certain fundamental problems of human existence—including the nature and meaning of life as well as the ways in which human identity is defined and maintained—and then to translate those answers into terms understandable to the questioner. Thus, according to Geertz (1973:14), the "aim of anthropology is the enlargement of the universe of human discourse." To accomplish that aim, symbolic anthropologists seek answers to a particular set of questions in the conduct of cultural analysis: "What are the conditions of existence? How is life defined? What kinds of units are specified and differentiated according to what assumptions or premises about the nature of the universe? How are these formulated, and how are they expressed?" (Dolgin, Kemnitzer, and Schneider 1977:20).

There is more to the paradigm than just the collection of emic data, however. Beyond the emic particulars of a thousand world views, symbolic anthropology searches for the etic universals of human nature and cultural process. "Our double task," writes Geertz, "is to uncover the conceptual structures that inform our subjects' acts . . . *and* to construct a system of analysis in whose terms what is generic to those structures, what belongs to them because they are what they are, will stand out against the other determinants of human behavior" (1973:27; emphasis added). "Enlarging the universe of human discourse" is a worthwhile goal, but the scientific merit of symbolic anthropology will depend ultimately upon how well the paradigm is able to carry out the second half of its "double task." At this stage, the preliminary results are promising, but final judgment must be reserved. Symbolic anthropology has so far produced disappointingly few theoretical principles to explain the universal characteristics of human nature and symbolic processes.

The epistemological principles of symbolic anthropology differ sharply from those of structuralism. Both paradigms ultimately offer analyses of the etics of thought—that is, both offer interpretations of what is going on inside the heads of their informants, and both paradigms begin their analyses with the examination of emic mental domains. But symbolic anthropologists, unlike structuralists, insist that the consistency and coherency of their etic mental interpretations are to be tested against emic mental and etic behavioral data. Both structuralists and symbolic anthropologists offer interpretations of domains of meaning, but, as Honigmann (1976:330) notes, structural "meaning" is an artifact of the method employed, whereas symbolic anthropological "meaning" is an artifact of the culture under study.

Symbolic anthropology's epistemological principles are naturally dependent upon its ontological premises. According to Geertz (1973:12), meaning is public because culture is public. Hence observation and inquiry are the fundamental epistemological procedures of symbolic anthropology. In an implicit criticism of structuralism, Geertz (ibid.:30) remarks that "nothing will discredit a semiotic approach to culture more quickly than allowing it to drift into . . . intuitionism . . . no matter how elegantly the intuitions are expressed." Symbolic anthropology is allied with cultural materialism in the "generalized attack on privacy theories of meaning" (ibid.:12). Undeniably, symbolic anthropologists know what they know by imaginative insight (ethnographic analysis, says Geertz (ibid.:9), consists of "sorting out the structures of signification"), but the imaginative insight of symbolic anthropologists is always vulnerable to empirical criticism. "Whatever, or wherever, symbolic systems . . . may be, we gain empirical access to them by inspecting events" (ibid.:17).

The question of "empirical access" is especially important because it lies at the heart of the difference between symbolic anthropology and structuralism. Parker (1985:64) is correct in pointing out that "Geertz has consistently characterized culture as a social phenomenon, or a shared system of intersubjective symbols and meanings." Indeed, Geertz (1986:373) reaffirms that position in his most recent work: "Whatever sense we have of how things stand with someone else's inner life, we gain it through their expressions, not through some magical intrusion into their consciousness." In the paradigm's stated logic, there is no possibility that the "meaning" identified by symbolic anthropological investigation exists only in the mind of the investigator.

In a memorable phrase, Geertz characterizes the work of symbolic anthropology as "thick description." Faced with the "multiplicity of complex conceptual structures," the symbolic anthropologist attempts "first to grasp [the meaning of those structures] and then to render [that meaning in terms understandable to the observer]" (Geertz 1973:10). Symbolic anthropologists maintain that all etic descriptions of meaning must be demonstrably grounded in emic reality and either elicitable or identifiable as part of the emic domain. The data-collecting activities of symbolic anthropologists—"interviewing informants, observing rituals, eliciting kin terms, tracing property lines, censusing households," and so on (ibid.:10)—are the same as those pursued by cultural materialists. In principle, then, symbolic anthropological analyses are replicable and self-correcting.

The theoretical principles of symbolic anthropology are, by the admission of symbolic anthropologists themselves, somewhat vague.

> A repertoire of very general, made-in-the-academy concepts and systems of concepts—"integration, "rationalization," "symbol," "ideology," "ethos," "revolution," "identity," "metaphor," "structure," "ritual," "world view," "actor," "function," "sacred," and, of course, "culture" itself—is woven into the body of thick-description ethnography in the hope of rendering mere occurrences scientifically eloquent (Geertz 1973:28).

Geertz (ibid.:20) declares that "cultural analysis is . . . guessing at the meanings, assessing the guesses, and drawing explanatory conclusions from the better guesses." However, with the exception of a few "very general concepts," symbolic anthropology does not specify what principles to employ when searching for explanatory conclusions.

The most important of those general concepts is the concept of culture. Following Geertz, symbolic anthropologists have adopted a definition of "culture" that is less encompassing than Tylor's "complex whole." Culture refers to "an historically transmitted pattern of meanings embodied in symbols, a system of inherited conceptions expressed in symbolic forms by means of which men communicate, perpetuate, and develop their knowledge about and attitudes toward life" (Geertz 1973:89). It is to this domain that symbolic anthropological explanations and interpretations are applied.

Despite the imprecision and relative paucity of its theoretical principles, symbolic anthropology does offer a well-defined and well-developed set of theoretical assumptions. Symbolic anthropologists share with all social scientists "the premise that social action tends to be orderly, to be, in some degree, predictable or understandable by both participants and observers" (Dolgin, Kemnitzer, and Schneider 1977:4). In addition, symbolic anthropologists assume that "life must have meaning [that is, people must assign meaning to it] . . . and that entails a system of signs or symbols in which this meaning is embodied and expressed" (ibid.:33). That "system of signs or symbols," of course, is what symbolic anthropologists mean by "culture." Symbolic anthropology derives its raison d'être from the assumption that "shared, or culturally constituted, meaning entails symbols which stand for something in some respect" (Dolgin, Kemnitzer, and Schneider 1977:18). Thus the fundamental assumption of symbolic anthropology is that "culture consists of socially established structures of meaning" (Geertz 1973:12), and the fundamental task of symbolic anthropology is to discover how symbols are created, structured, and used.

There are other assumptions and concepts associated with symbolic anthropology as well. One is Victor Turner's (1969) notion of the "multivocalic" character of symbols, or the capacity of symbols to represent several different meanings at once. Another is the concept, also prominent in the work of Turner, of the processual character of social systems. Symbolic anthropologists assume that symbols play a critical role in sociocultural process. Turner, for example, argues that "even in the simplest societies, the distinction between structure [the hierarchical order of social, political, and economic statuses and roles] and communitas [the direct, unmediated, and unstructured communion of individual persons] exists and obtains symbolic expression in the cultural attributes of liminality, marginality, and inferiority" and that, taken together, structure and communitas "constitute the 'human condition,' as regards man's relations with his fellow man" (1969:130). For symbolic anthropologists such as Turner, all societies are ongoing processes of the dialectic between structure and communitas (ibid.:139). Even among those symbolic anthropologists who do not subscribe to a processual model of society, there is general agreement that "sociocultural systems depend not only for their meaning but also for their existence upon the participation of *conscious* human agents" (Turner 1974:17; emphasis in original).

The explanations offered by symbolic anthropologists are explicitly interpretive. For Geertz (1973:5), the analysis of culture is "not an experimental science in search of law but an interpretive one in search of meaning." Grasping and rendering emic realities is necessarily an interpretive exercise. According to Geertz (1977:492), "Understanding the form and pressure of . . . natives' inner lives is more like grasping a proverb, catching an illusion, [or] seeing a joke." In that sense, symbolic anthropology is similar to structuralism, which also offers interpretive explanations, and is distinct from cultural materialism, which offers causal explanations.

The relative commensurability or incommensurability of cultural materialism, structuralism, and symbolic anthropology requires a further comment. I have said that paradigms are commensurable to the extent that they share a common problem and specify a similar means of solution. By that measure cultural materialism obviously is incommensurable with both structuralism and symbolic anthropology (see Scholte 1966). Obviously, too, structuralism and symbolic anthropology are more closely related. Although one is concerned with the structure of the human mind and the other is concerned with the psychological and sociocultural significance of meaning, both paradigms touch ultimately upon the common problem of human nature. Structuralism and symbolic anthropology, however, specify different means of solution and have radically different ontological and epistemological assumptions and principles. Paradigmatic commensurability is a relative matter. Structuralism and symbolic anthropology are relatively incommensurable. Whereas structuralism aims to discover the universal cognitive processes by which human beings assign meaning to and derive meaning from their experiences, symbolic anthropology attempts to discover the universal cultural processes by which humans do so. Although structuralism and symbolic anthropology are both concerned with the problem of meaning, they approach that problem from different tacks. From a scientific viewpoint, symbolic anthropological interpretations are preferable to structuralist interpretations because the former appeal to external factors for verification.

Symbolic anthropology and cultural materialism, on the other hand, are incommensurable but not necessarily incompatible (see Shankman

1984:277). The causal explanations offered by cultural materialism and the interpretive explanations offered by symbolic anthropology do not necessarily (and, in fact, do not usually) contradict one another, although cultural materialism and other varieties of "cognitive anthropology" are often contradictory. Symbolic anthropology and ethnoscience are not the same, however. According to Harris (1979:265), "Cognitivism . . . is a strategy for describing in the most effective and emically authentic fashion the rules or other mental programs that allegedly account for behavior." Symbolic anthropologists are allied with cultural materialists in rejecting that theoretical approach. Geertz (1973:18) affirms that "code does not determine conduct," and he recognizes the "cognitive fallacy" that culture consists simply of the rules one needs to know to behave as a native (ibid.:11–12). According to Geertz (ibid.:14), "Culture is not a [causal] power. . . . It is a context." Harris's (1979:258–286) critique of "cognitive idealism" is well conceived, but he makes only very brief reference to symbolic anthropology (ibid.:281–282) and then only to note symbolic anthropology's "intense commitment to cultural idealist principles." But an interest in the study of ideational domains, as I have attempted to demonstrate, is not necessarily a commitment to idealist determinism. Symbolic anthropology is not cognitive idealism.

Nor can symbolic anthropology be dismissed as "unscientific" simply because its explanations are interpretive rather than causal. Structuralism is unscientific not because its explanations are interpretive but because its explanations are invulnerable to empirical criticism. Science explains phenomena by subsuming them under some general covering law, but that does not mean that science necessarily adduces causal explanations. To equate science with causal explanations is to confuse a method of inquiry with a variety of explanation. There are other scientific laws besides laws of causality, including laws of covariance. As discussed in Chapter 2, unremitting criticism and empirical vulnerability are the essential attributes of the scientific approach.

Many critics—and, to be fair, many symbolic anthropologists themselves—continue to believe that the scientific and interpretive approaches are mutually exclusive. Paul Shankman (1984:261), for example, claims that "the programmatic side of Geertz's work is an attempt to refocus anthropology—indeed all of social science—away from the emulation of the natural sciences and toward a reintegration with the humanities." I think Shankman is correct, but only in the most superficial sense. Certainly it is true that symbolic anthropology "draws its inspiration from the arts and the humanities rather than the natural sciences proper," as Scholte (1984b:542) says, but although the validity of an interpretive explanation is generally associated with its capacity to compel assent, there is no inherent reason that interpretive explanations cannot appeal to scientific standards of verification. As long as interpretive explanations are systematic, consistent, coherent, replicable, and falsifiable, they are scientific. What Geertz means by "interpretive" explanations, Hempel would call "inductive-statistical" explanations. The interpretive explanations offered by symbolic anthropologists appeal, even if implicitly, to inductive covering laws. If symbolic anthropology would make its epistemological principles more explicit and uncompromising, the paradigm could definitively preclude interpretations that fail to meet the criteria of science.

The essential weakness of symbolic anthropology is not that it fails to account for the causes of human thought and behavior, as cultural materialists argue. Instead, the most significant deficiency of symbolic anthropology is its lack of explicit theoretical and methodological guidelines, to which I have alluded. There are three aspects to this problem of theoretical and methodological imprecision.

First, there is the problem of replicability. If one lacks the imaginative insight of Clifford Geertz, how is one to pursue research under the paradigm of symbolic anthropology? The paradigm itself offers few clues. In fact, Geertz (1983:11) implies that those who wish to carry out symbolic analyses will simply have to learn the methodology on their own because the successful practice of the interpretive approach is "one of those things like riding a bicycle that is easier done than said." In a critique of symbolic anthropology, Renner (1984:540) observes that "the absence of an empirically convincing theory and methodology has as its consequence the fact that there can be no program for the direction in which research should proceed."

Second, there is the problem of verification, which symbolic anthropologists recognize. Geertz (1973:24) correctly observes that "the besetting sin of interpretive approaches . . . is that they tend to resist, or to be permitted to resist, conceptual articulation and thus to escape systematic modes of assessment." Even Geertz's sympathetic critics agree with him about the shortcomings of interpretive paradigms. Richardson (1984:275), for example, writes that "to be sure, interpretive social science has its own risks: of being overly precious, of being obscure, of turning a thick interpretation into a dense one. The issue of verification is indeed important."

Structural analysis fails to come to grips with this issue, and, as a result, structural explanations are presented as self-validating. Geertz recognizes, however, that "there is no reason why the conceptual structure of a cultural interpretation . . . [should not be] susceptible to explicit canons of appraisal" (Geertz 1973:24). Yet at the same time he argues that the unique nature of cultural interpretation limits the anthropologist's ability to specify such standards of appraisal. He suggests that cultural understanding is incremental and dependent upon successively more "incisive" interpretations, but that the standards of "incisiveness" defy explicit formulation. Superior interpretations, he maintains, are characterized simply by "greater precision and broader relevance."

Geertz's argument is not compelling. There is no inherent quality in the interpretive analysis of culture that necessarily precludes the establishment of rigorous standards of authenticity. A given interpretive analysis should be consistent with the "facts" of the world and with the common body of theory upon which all related interpretations are based. Assuming that a given interpretive explanation is falsifiable and unfalsified, it can be considered true if it explains the phenomenon in question more comprehensively, coherently, and cogently than any of its competitors. It is incumbent upon symbolic anthropologists to construct an explicit and coherent body of explanatory principles capable of generating such explanations.

The third aspect of this problem of theoretical insufficiency is the looming specter of archinductivism. Symbolic anthropologists frequently and erroneously assume that the mere accumulation of emic data eventually will reveal significant theoretical principles that explain cross-cultural commonalities. The "double task" of symbolic anthropology—analyzing the symbolic properties of emic semantic domains and constructing analytic principles to explain etic cultural processes—will remain forever half-finished until explicit theories are formulated and tested to explain those etic processes. Symbolic anthropologists have not completed that task, but, in all fairness, it is one they have begun and begun well, although some critics have charged that interpretive anthropologists have lately turned away from that endeavor (Shankman 1984:269).

The great strength of symbolic anthropology, in fact, lies in the cogency of the paradigm's etic generalizations and explanations. Symbolic anthropologists have contributed valuable insights about the nature and significance of symbolic realms. Among the compelling concepts emanating from symbolic anthropology is the distinction between "world view" and "ethos." Geertz (1973:126–141) defines "world view" as the "assumed structure of reality," or the culturally specific set of existential assumptions, and "ethos" as the "approved style of life," or the socially established set of normative precepts. In all cultures, Geertz argues, people draw normative conclusions from factual premises and vice versa. He suggests that religion, a recognized cultural universal, invariably fuses world view and ethos and derives its cultural legitimacy from the aura of authenticity engendered by that fusion. Geertz concludes that "the tendency to synthesize world view and ethos at some level, if not logically necessary, is at least empirically coercive; if it is not philosophically justified, it is at least pragmatically universal" (ibid.:127).

(The universal fusion of world view and ethos is an example of a well-substantiated, inductive-statistical covering law.) Cross-culturally, the fusion of world view and ethos usually is accomplished with little regard for logical consistency, although logical inconsistency does not seem to hamper the effectiveness of that fusion. The ethos of Catholicism, for example, has undergone enormous changes in the past five hundred years while the Catholic world view has remained relatively unchanged, yet Catholicism continues to play an important role in numerous sociocultural systems throughout the world. Geertz's analysis of the relation between world view and ethos illustrates the promise of symbolic anthropology, for it is an analysis that reveals something profound and fundamental about human nature while at the same time revealing an unsuspected and significant aspect of sociocultural process (namely, that although superstructural components explain, rationalize, and abet infrastructural conditions, they do not do so in any logically consistent or rational way). The notion of the multivocality of symbols is a similarly seminal concept. Geertz (1973:141) observes that "the role of such a special science as anthropology in the analysis of values is not to replace philosophical investigation, but to make it relevant."

At this stage in the development of symbolic anthropology, it would be premature to come to a final conclusion about the merits of the paradigm. Some analysts, such as Shankman (1984:269), are uncertain about the paradigm's prospects—"there is no clear future for interpretive theory"—while others, such as Rice (1980:250), argue that the limits of the research strategy remain to be discovered—"the debate over the merits of Geertz's approach definitely remains an open-ended one." Still other commentators are more laudatory. Scholte (1984b:542) regards symbolic anthropology as a praiseworthy alternative to "the reductionism and ethnocentrism of traditional science"; Richardson (1984:275) sees an ethical or aesthetic value in the paradigm—"the interpretive approach, by combining the social with the cultural, power with poetry, directs us towards the task of making anthropology, the science of humanity, a truly human science." As for myself, I am appreciative of the paradigm's contributions, attracted by its aesthetics, impressed by its potential, and concerned about its lack of rigor.

Suggestions for Further Reading

The paradigm of symbolic anthropology receives its fullest expression in the work of Clifford Geertz, particularly in *The Interpretation of Cultures* (1973) and *Local Knowledge* (1983). '*As People Express Their Lives, So They Are . . .*' is an edited volume (Dolgin, Kemnitzer, and Schneider 1977) reflecting the range of symbolic anthropology.

For a representative collection of articles illustrating the paradigmatic approach of symbolic anthropology, see Shweder and LeVine (1984) and Turner and Bruner (1986). The paradigm has also had an impact among archeologists; for a sample of that work, see Hodder (1982).

13

The Question of Paradigmatic Commitment

Until such time as science is practiced by something other than human scientists, it will never be totally dispassionate, but this fact hardly invalidates the scientific way of knowing. Science remains our best hope for discovering "objective" truth about the empirical world. But it does mean that the role of values in the conduct of science should be examined explicitly. The choice among cultural materialism, structuralism, and symbolic anthropology must be made not only with consideration of each paradigm's intrinsic merit, but with due regard for the question of value as well. By the selection of a paradigm, scientists indicate which questions they find most important, significant, timely, convenient, useful, politic, or simply attractive. As Levi-Strauss (1976:ix) aptly notes, "What is interesting in man is not subject to scientific decision but results and always will result from a choice which is ultimately of a philosophical order."

Cultural materialism, structuralism, and symbolic anthropology are each associated with a particular set of values. I want to describe briefly what I perceive those values to be, but I want to qualify my observations first: I do not claim that I have described fully the various and complex set of moral and ethical propositions underlying these various research strategies, nor that all cultural materialists, structuralists, or symbolic anthropologists necessarily or invariably profess any or all of the values I perceive to be associated with each paradigm. Instead, I simply am suggesting what seem to me to be the broad outlines of those value positions, and I offer as evidence the statements of those most notably associated with each paradigm.

Cultural materialism, according to its principal proponent (Harris 1979:158), "inevitably contributes to a radical critique of the status quo." Gans (1985) perceptively notes that the value for "egalitarianism" lies at the heart of cultural materialism's theoretical principles. As far as Harris (1979:75) is concerned, rival paradigms should be evaluated according to their "respective ability to solve puzzles pertaining to socially significant issues." By "socially significant issues," cultural materialists mean such things as poverty, underdevelopment, imperialism, the population explosion, ethnic and class conflict, exploitation, political repression, crime, war, and the like (Harris 1979:285). For cultural materialists, the anthropological investigation of the human experience should necessarily center upon such issues. According to the values that underlie cultural materialism, the failure to address these important questions would be tantamount to an abrogation of moral responsibility.

Structuralists, in contrast, regard anthropology as an essentially introspective activity. Levi-Strauss (1976:ix) says that "the subject of the human sciences is man, yet the man who studies himself as he practices the human sciences will always allow his preferences to interfere in the way he defines himself to himself." According to the principal proponent of structuralism, then, self-knowledge is the ultimate result and the final goal of structural analysis. Structuralists are not interested in making scientific contributions to the "betterment" of the world, whatever that might mean. "It may be objected that this kind of science can scarcely be of much practical effect. The answer to this is that its main purpose is not a practical one. It meets intellectual requirements rather than or instead of satisfying needs" (Levi-Strauss 1966:9). According to Levi-Strauss (ibid.), "Classifying . . . has a value of its own." Structuralists place preeminent value upon the intellectual satisfactions derived from rational inquiry.

Symbolic anthropologists are attracted to and fascinated by the intricately developed semantic systems of human cultures. That is to say, symbolic anthropologists typically have "humanistic" interests, as the term is popularly used. Turner (1969:3) observes that "man's 'imaginative' and 'emotional' life is always and everywhere rich and complex." This proposition is scarcely debatable and would be embraced readily by virtually every other anthropological paradigm. For symbolic anthropologists, however, aesthetic analyses of "man's imaginative and emotional life" have their own satisfactions and are their own justification. Other anthropological paradigms are less concerned with such aesthetic perspectives, to the dismay of symbolic anthropologists such as Turner (1974:17): "I would plead with my colleagues to acquire the humanistic skills that would enable them to live more comfortably in those territories where the masters of human thought and art have long been dwelling. This must be done if a unified science of man, an authentic anthropology, is ever to become possible."

An abiding respect and affection for the inventiveness and imagination of the human species underlie all of symbolic anthropology's statements and premises. Turner, for example, says he regards "mankind as one in essence though manifold in expression, *creative* and not merely adaptive in his manifoldness" (1974:17; emphasis added). In a criticism of cultural materialism that carries more emotive than propositional force, Dolgin, Kemnitzer and Schneider (1977:7) argue that Harris's "notion of anthropology loses the critical edge which an inquiry into belief, ideology, and freedom could have."

Which of these paradigms is associated with the most defensible value position? Should anthropology be a source of social criticism, a mirror for personal reflection, or a vehicle for aesthetic analysis and cross-cultural understanding? Each anthropologist must answer that question on a personal basis, but I for one would not object to anthropology's being all three. These particular sets of values are not necessarily contradictory, except as the adoption of one may preclude the adoption of the others, but, from the perspective of the discipline as a whole, there is no reason why these three different values should not exist in complementary distribution. Certainly it is important for anthropology to offer informed critiques of the world. If it did not do so, anthropology would be more an instrument of political propaganda than a science of the human condition. But it is equally certain that anthropology should be concerned with the problem of human nature. The quest for self-knowledge demands an anthropological contribution. I am not persuaded that the investigation of "intellectual" problems should await the solution of "practical" problems. The world is unlikely ever to be saved.

I would quibble with particular aspects of each paradigm's set of values (it is important, for example, to eventually distinguish between emic and etic realities despite symbolic anthropology's contention that it is heuristically sufficient to treat emic realities as "real"), but I cannot recommend or reject commitment to any of these three paradigms solely on the basis of value. All three paradigms address valuable questions. Two of them, cultural materialism and symbolic anthropology, do so in a reasonably coherent and authentic fashion. The third, structuralism, has undeniable intellectual appeal although its scientific merit is dubious. Which paradigm to choose ultimately becomes a question of which problem to address. In the final analysis, it is a question of research design.

Cultural materialism, structuralism, and symbolic anthropology each consider the investigation of their respective sets of problems to be the essential task of anthropology. Each is mistaken. The essential task of anthropology is not simply to explain the causes of sociocultural similarities and differences, or to discover the structure of human thought processes, or to analyze the significance of meaning in and for human life, but to comprehend the human experience. Anthropology must account for the maintenance of human life and the maintenance of human identity. These problems assuredly are interrelated, but anthropology has yet to produce a single integrative paradigm that treats them in a fully satisfactory manner. Invariably, anthropological paradigms have tended to focus upon aspects and implications of one problem or the other. Cultural materialism, structuralism, and symbolic anthropology are no exception. Levi-Strauss (1966:3) says that "the universe is an object of thought at least as much as it is a means of satisfying needs," but structuralism, along with symbolic anthropology, treats the universe primarily as an object of thought and largely ignores the universe as a means of satisfying needs. Cultural materialism is less restrictive of the problems that fall within its domain of inquiry, but cultural materialists certainly do not give equal attention to these two problems. Cultural materialism's "socially significant issues" are raised by people's efforts to satisfy their physical needs.

The conclusion to which this analysis has been building is that cultural materialism is the best paradigm yet developed to address the problems associated with the maintenance of human life, while symbolic anthropology is the best paradigm yet developed to address the problems associated with the maintenance of human identity. I am suggesting, then, a very purposeful and deliberate kind of eclecticism. One of the most significant challenges facing contemporary anthropology is to address appropriate questions with appropriate theories. The maintenance of human life and the maintenance of human identity are interrelated problems; if cultural materialism and symbolic anthropology are to offer complementary explanations, it is essential that they do not advance conflicting explanations in the areas where those two problems overlap. To avoid that pitfall, anthropologists must be unequivocally clear and precise about the definition of problems and the application of paradigms.

Unfortunately, such clarity and precision are not characteristic of contemporary anthropology. Symbolic anthropologists and cultural materialists alike frequently fail to recognize the incommensurability of their respective approaches. Symbolic anthropologists, for example, have claimed that "there is nothing more 'down to earth' or 'basic' about kinship, economics, or status changes than there is about rituals [because] all occur only in societies and are first and foremost sociocultural activities" (Dolgin, Kemnitzer, and Schneider 1977:36). It is critical, however, to be clear about the meaning of such terms as "down to earth" and "basic." If we are considering peoples' perceptions of the sociocultural world, then religion and economics may be equally "down to earth." But if we are talking about cultural causality, then infrastructural components are more "basic" than superstructural ones. Paradigmatic comparisons, whether implicit or explicit, are all too often more emotive than propositional. Dolgin, Kemnitzer, and Schneider (ibid.:6) are simply confused and confusing when they say "we feel the influence of any kind of 'external' facts on human actions is easily overemphasized." Cultural materialists are similarly confused when they equate studies of the ideational realm with ideational determinism.

It might be objected that anthropology would be better served by a single paradigm that integrated the problems of human life and human identity, and, indeed, I would agree in principle with that objection. Scientific progress undoubtedly will result when some innovative theorist is able to address both problems from a single comprehensive theoretical perspective. In the meantime, anthropology is no more handicapped by the coexistence of two complementary paradigms than contemporary physics is handicapped by its failure to integrate nuclear, electromagnetic, and gravitational forces in a unified field theory. Developing an analogous "unified field theory" for the domain of human experience is one of the future challenges of anthropology. The anthropological challenge of the moment is to refine and extend cultural materialism and symbolic anthropology, to explore the limits of each paradigm's explanatory power, and to evaluate the cogency of these two paradigms with respect to their competitors. This last task is made especially difficult by the paradigmatic imprecision of much anthropological research, analysis, and discussion. As we shall see in Part 4, contemporary anthropologists sometimes sail into paradigmatic debates with little understanding of what their opponents are trying to say. Paradigmatic clashes in anthropology are often noisy affairs, but all too often they have all the significance of ships that pass in the night.

Suggestions for Further Reading

In *Cultural Materialism,* Marvin Harris (1979) comes to a conclusion very different from the one presented in this chapter; for still another point of view, see *The End of Culture,* by Eric Gans (1985).

PART FOUR

THE CLASH
OF PARADIGMS

To the extent . . . that two scientific schools disagree about what is a problem and what a solution, they will inevitably talk through each other when debating the relative merits of their respective paradigms.
—Thomas Kuhn,
The Structure of Scientific Revolutions

14

The Sound
and the Fury

I have said that the unique value of the scientific approach stems in large part from the fact that science is practiced by a critical community of scientists. The errors of observation or interpretation made by individual scientists ideally are corrected by their colleagues in an unrelenting process of scrutiny and review. Thus it is crucial for scientists to understand the nature of paradigmatic inquiry. Any particular observation or explanation is the product of a particular paradigm and must be critiqued as such. Scientists unfamiliar with the notion of paradigmatic incommensurability will be unable to evaluate scientific accounts produced under the auspices of paradigms to which they themselves are not committed. Inevitably, such scientists will compare and evaluate all rival theories as though those theories had been produced by paradigms commensurable with their own research strategies. As I have explained, incommensurable paradigms must be compared and evaluated in a manner different from that employed to evaluate commensurable paradigms. The failure of many contemporary anthropologists to recognize that fact is a significant shortcoming of the discipline and one that threatens to undermine the scientific validity of anthropology.

I think I can illustrate the dangers associated with the failure to recognize the occasional incommensurability of paradigms by reference to a hypothetical example. Imagine, if you will, two anthropologists who intend to study the ritual behavior of a particular culture. The first is a visual anthropologist; he wants to study decorative motifs, spatial relations, lighting techniques, patterns of movement, and similar phenomena when he observes the ritual in question. The second is an aural anthropologist; she wants to study liturgical chants, musical effects, oratory styles, extraneous conversation, and the like when she arrives on the scene.

The visual anthropologist conducts his research under the auspices of a paradigm that involves the use of a camera. He declares that the research problem in which he is interested is the making of a complete photographic record of the ritual. His research strategy is to take as many different pictures from as many different angles as possible.

The aural anthropologist pursues her research under the auspices of a paradigm that involves the use of a tape recorder. She declares that the research problem she wants to tackle is the making of a complete audio record of the event. Her research strategy is to make as many different recordings with as many different microphones as possible.

When the visual and aural anthropologists confront one another in the journals of their discipline, they fail to recognize the incommensurability of their paradigmatic approaches. The visual anthropologist insists that his camera takes better pictures than his rival's tape recorder; the aural anthropologist adamantly maintains that her tape recorder makes far better sound recordings than her competitor's camera. The visual anthropologist steadfastly defends his paradigm; his 35 mm, single lens reflex, fully automatic camera represents a considerable improvement over the instamatic cameras used by fieldworkers in years gone by. Moreover, the visual anthropologist designed the camera's shoulder strap himself, and he cites the article in which he first claimed that innovation. The aural anthropologist is unimpressed; after all, her miniature cassette recorder not only has a built-in tape counter but is capable of recording with or without a hand-held microphone. Furthermore, she developed the system of labeling cassette tapes that has been adopted by virtually every anthropologist working in Micronesia, and she cites the article that establishes that fact.

So it goes. The visual anthropologist faults the aural anthropologist because she has neglected to analyze the proxemics of the ritual, while the aural anthropologist chastises the visual anthropologist because he failed to notice the highly significant tonal differences in the utterances of the priests and the communicants. The two anthropologists talk past one another. They fail to evaluate each other's claims in a responsible, scientific fashion because they fail to understand what claims each is making. Their approaches are completely incommensurable—they specify different problems for investigation (one wants to make a photographic record, the other an audio record), and they specify different means of solution (one advocates the use of a camera; the other calls for the use of a tape recorder).

To pursue this analogy briefly, imagine that the two anthropologists remain loyal to their preferred methods of solution but now specify a common problem: Each declares that he or she wants to make as complete a record as possible of the entire ritual activity. Now they have some common ground for discussion. The visual anthropologist can argue that his pictures capture the most significant aspects of the event, and the aural anthropologist can argue that her recordings encapsulate the essence of the activity. Both, in other words, can claim to solve the problem more efficaciously. In this case, their two approaches are only relatively incommensurable; they can be compared directly if the two anthropologists can reach some agreement regarding the real importance or significance of ritual activity. Both, of course, are vulnerable to the innovative theorist who will suggest that a videotape recorder be used to solve the problem.

The visual anthropologist and the aural anthropologist can evaluate each other's work, even if they specify completely different research problems. In fact, they must do so if they wish to be scientists. But to say that a camera takes better pictures than a tape recorder is absurd. Instead, the visual anthropologist must argue that the aural anthropologist does not solve the problems she defined for herself; or that her method of solution is unscientific, unfalsifiable, or falsified; or that it is more important, for some demonstrable or arguable reason, to have photographic records of rituals rather than audio records.

This hypothetical example is admittedly a caricature. Paradigmatic debate in anthropology (or any discipline for that matter) is invariably more complex. The distinction between the visual anthropologist and his aural colleague is essentially a methodological one; the distinctions between actual paradigms are almost always less simple and more subtle, involving ontological, epistemological, and theoretical differences as well as methodological ones. What I intend to illustrate with this analogy is simply the fact that the proponents of competing paradigms very often tend to talk past one another when debating the merits of their respective positions. The debate between the visual and the aural anthropologist is characterized by a high degree of absurdity, and that comedic element unfortunately is present in much of the actual paradigmatic debate that takes place in anthropology.

In the next two chapters, I intend to substantiate these points by closely examining a pair of actual paradigmatic debates in contemporary anthropology. Both debates involve clashes between cultural determinists and cultural materialists. Neither paradigm will emerge blameless from the analysis that follows.

For a variety of reasons, contemporary paradigmatic clashes often involve cultural materialists, who tend to be concerned most explicitly with issues of paradigmatic commitment. Cultural materialists frequently compare their paradigm with its competitors, and, like the visual anthropologist who insisted that no other paradigm produced pictures as good as those produced by his camera, cultural materialists frequently beg the question when making a case for their paradigm. Ross (1980), for example, argues that no other paradigm explains the causes of sociocultural differences and similarities as well as cultural materialism. Harris (1979:296–297) criticizes "the eclectic strategy" for being "a highly inefficient way to study the causes of sociocultural differences and similarities." Price (1982:735) observes correctly that "theoretical propositions must be tested against each other as well as against data and evaluated on metatheoretical as well as empirical grounds," but she offers that observation after having tested cultural materialism's rivals "in the analysis of certain problems of similarity and difference, stability and change in cultural systems" (ibid.). Many of cultural materialism's competitors, however, do not address themselves to those problems. Cultural materialism's rivals cannot be faulted simply because they are not cultural materialism. Goldschmidt (1983:698) is not alone in decrying "the unnecessary negativism that characterizes the stance of cultural materialism" and in criticizing the "posturing" of many cultural materialists.

To be fair, it should be noted that cultural materialism's detractors frequently fault cultural materialism simply for being cultural materialism. Muriel Dimen-Schein (1977:xv), for example, says that she rebelled against the "quite rigid, materialist, determinist view of culture and human evolution" she was taught in graduate school because that view "cannot account for or explain how cultural ideology, through individual consciousness or subjectivity, results in the individual action." Dimen-Schein apparently fails to recognize that the question she would like answered is not one that cultural materialism is especially interested in addressing. Manners and Kaplan (1968:10) aptly note that anthropological theories sometimes "function as ideologies, and the reaction to them is often in terms of their ideological rather than their scientific implications."

The two paradigmatic debates discussed in the following chapters involve issues that are familiar to most contemporary anthropologists: the world view of peasants and the sanctity of India's cattle. These two issues have been the center of remarkably contentious discussion, and, unfortunately, most anthropologists who have participated in the debates have failed to recognize the incommensurability of the paradigms involved.

Suggestions for Further Reading

The issue of paradigmatic commensurability in anthropology is not one that many anthropologists have addressed; a notable exception is Bob Scholte (1966; 1980). Marvin Harris (1979), of course, takes a different point of view on anthropological paradigms in *Cultural Materialism*.

15

The Image
of Limited Good

The debate surrounding the nature of the world view of peasants is, more than anything else, a debate between cultural determinists and cultural materialists. In Part 3, I noted that cultural determinism seeks to explain why people think and behave the way they do, while cultural materialism tries to explain how different systems of thought and behavior come into being. The basic theoretical principle of cultural determinism holds that individual behavior is determined by cultural influence; the fundamental theoretical principle of cultural materialism maintains that cultural patterns of belief and behavior are determined by infrastructural variables. One paradigm asks, "What determines behavior?" and answers, "Culture." The other asks, "What determines culture?" and answers, "Infrastructure." It will be important to keep in mind the differences and incommensurability between cultural determinism and cultural materialism in the discussion that follows.

George Foster (1965; 1979) devised the concept of the "image of limited good" to characterize the world view of peasants in the Mexican village of Tzintzuntzan, although he argued that the concept applied as well to peasants throughout the world. According to Foster, peasants were envious, suspicious, and fatalistic and assumed the structure of reality precludes happiness and satisfaction for all but a very few people:

> By *Image of Limited Good* I mean that behavior . . . is patterned in such
> a fashion as to suggest that Tzintzuntzenos see their social, economic,
> and natural universes—their total environment—as one in which almost
> all desired things in life such as land, other forms of wealth, health,
> friendship, love, manliness, honor, respect, power, influence, security, and
> safety *exist in absolute quantities insufficient to fill even minimal needs of
> villagers.* Not only do "good things" exist in strictly limited quantities,
> but in addition *there is no way directly within the Tzintzuntzeno's power to
> increase the available supplies.* . . . "Good," like land, is seen as something
> inherent in nature, there to be divided and redivided if necessary, to be
> passed around, but not to be augmented (1979:123–124; emphasis in
> original).

In effect, Foster offered an emic account of the world view of
Tzintzuntzenos as a particular illustration of the etic generalization that
thought and behavior are determined by culture. Foster was (and is) a
quintessential cultural determinist. He did not concern himself, except
tangentially, with the factors that brought the Tzintzuntzeno world view
into being. Foster's analysis was aimed at the nature of the peasant
world view, not the cause of that world view.

> In treating of the way in which people look at the world, two levels of
> analysis are involved. On the one hand we are concerned with *description*,
> for by observing how people act a cognitive orientation can be learned.
> . . . On the other hand we are concerned with the problem of an economical
> *representation* of this cognitive orientation by means of models or other
> devices which account for observed behavior and which permit prediction
> of behavior as yet unnoted or unperformed (ibid.:122–123; emphasis in
> original).

When Foster said that the image of limited good "accounts for observed
behavior," he meant individual behavior, not systems of behavior. He
was not claiming that the peasant world view determined the nature
of the peasant economy; instead, he was explaining how and why
individual Tzintzuntzenos perceived the world the way they did. For
Foster, individual behavior was the product of cultural influence, and
the image of limited good was one component of Mexican peasant
culture. When Foster did touch upon the question of the causes of the
image of limited good, he invariably pointed to the existence of material
constraints.

> For the underlying, fundamental truth is that in an economy like Tzin-
> tzuntzan's, hard work and thrift are moral qualities of only the slightest
> functional value. Because of the limitations on land and technology,

additional hard work does not produce a significant increment in income.
It is pointless to talk of thrift in a subsistence economy, because usually
there is no surplus with which to be thrifty. Foresight, with careful planning
for the future, is also a virtue of dubious value in a world in which the
best laid plans must rest on a foundation of chance and capriciousness
(ibid.:150).

In short, there was nothing in Foster's concept of the image of limited
good that contradicted the theoretical principles of cultural materialism.
Nothing about Foster's concept, of course, explicitly furthered the development or articulation of cultural materialism, and cultural materialists
may well be able to argue, with some justification, that cultural determinist
explanations are fairly unenlightening. But cultural materialists consistently have misinterpreted Foster, and they have insisted that Foster's
arguments are contradicted by cultural materialist principles.

James Acheson (1972) launched the first of the cultural materialist
attacks against the image of limited good in an article entitled "Limited
Good or Limited Goods? Response to Economic Opportunity in a Tarascan
Pueblo." The article presented an argument that can be understood only
if one assumes that Acheson was unfamiliar with the notion of paradigmatic incommensurability and, consequently, unable to properly evaluate incommensurable approaches. Acheson (ibid.:1152) maintained "that
blocks to development are primarily economic in nature, not cultural
or cognitive (e.g., 'limited good') as has been claimed by others working
in the area." Acheson (ibid.) went on to claim that "Foster ascribes this
inability to change primarily to the cognitive orientation of the people
of the Tarascan area, which he sums up with the concept of 'limited
good.'" This was simply not true. Foster did not ascribe the inability
to change primarily to cognitive factors; in fact, Foster only dealt with
change tangentially and then pointed to a combination of "psychological,
social, cultural, economic, and technological factors" that promote and
retard change (Foster 1979:250).

However, Foster failed to understand what Acheson meant by determinative causal factors or "primary responsibility" for change because
Foster did not understand Acheson's paradigm. Thus Foster must bear
part of the responsibility for the confusion because he, too, was unable
to properly evaluate incommensurable approaches. In a reply to Acheson,
Foster (1974:54) admitted that "it is true that I have found a good deal
of the inability of Tzintzuntzenos to take advantage of new opportunities
to be rooted in personality and social factors." But that is "true" only
in a cultural determinist sense; Foster meant that individual behavior
is determined by cultural influence. If individuals persist in maintaining
the same cognitive orientations, he argued, they will be unable to take

advantage of new opportunities. Foster's apparent admission of the "primacy" of personality factors was not "true" in Acheson's cultural materialist sense. Ask Foster what must happen in order to change the cognitive orientation, which in effect is what Acheson did, and Foster invariably will answer that the material conditions of life must first change. In other words, when new opportunities present themselves, most individuals will not maintain their old cognitive orientations (Foster emphasized that those who do take advantage of the new opportunities will change their outlooks). In that sense, Foster recognized that the inability of Tzintzuntzenos to change is rooted in material factors. Even innovative people, Foster declared (1979:251), will be unable to implement their innovations without a "fully developed infrastructure to train them and support them in their efforts." Establish such an infrastructure, Foster suggested, and innovative people will appear. So what was the argument about?

The argument was and continues to be about paradigms. Acheson thought Foster was guilty of cultural idealism and wanted Foster to be a consistent cultural materialist. Foster thought Acheson was guilty of economic reductionism and wanted Acheson to be a holistic cultural determinist. In his reply to Acheson, Foster (1974) insisted that the image of limited good was a true and accurate description of the world view of Mexican peasants (or at least between 1945 and 1965). But Acheson never quibbled with that point. In his reply to Foster, Acheson (1974:59) said that he was not questioning whether Mexican peasants were suspicious, just "the degree to which suspicion hinders development." But Foster never argued that cognitive orientations were more significant inhibitors of development than material conditions. Foster and Acheson failed completely to understand one another's paradigmatic assumptions and as a result succeeded only in talking past one another.

In his original critique of Foster, Acheson (1972:1153) wrote that although "a certain amount of data on technical and economic limitations" appears in Foster's work, "such factors have not received their proper weight in this discussion." In other words, Foster's chief sin was that he had not investigated the problems in which Acheson was interested. It is possible to attack an incommensurable paradigm on the grounds that its problems are unimportant, but such an attack must demonstrate why those problems are insignificant. It is pointless to argue that a paradigm is inadequate simply because it fails to address its incommensurable rival's problems. Acheson made that mistake because he was not aware of the paradigm Foster employed. As a result, Acheson interpreted all of Foster's statements as though they had been made by a wayward cultural materialist. "It is one thing to say that Tarascans are suspicious, distrustful, and uncooperative," Acheson (ibid.:1165) argued, but "it is another to assume that this lack of cooperation precludes all possibility for positive economic change." Foster never made such a claim, and when Foster (1974) attempted to say so, Acheson (1974:58) decided that Foster had undergone "a major change in his own thinking concerning development."

Foster, however, was guilty of similarly restrictive interpretations. Failing to realize that Acheson was working with a different set of paradigmatic premises, Foster interpreted all of Acheson's statements as though they had been made by a wayward cultural determinist. Foster's basic working hypothesis was that behavior is determined by culture, and he imagined that Acheson was attempting to reduce culture to mere economic factors: "Our 'existing body of theory' to explain these changes certainly needs modification and extension which will come *not from simplistic economic explanations alone*, but from careful, cautious, and broadly based analyses of all the economic, political, historical, social and psychological factors that are at play in modern Mexico" (Foster 1974:57; emphasis added). As we shall see in the context of the sacred cow controversy, cultural determinists frequently respond with emotive calls for "more fieldwork" when their theoretical positions are challenged.

The debate about the image of limited good did not end with the Acheson-Foster exchange, however. Harris (1979:297–300) argued that Foster's description and defense of the image of limited good were replete with internal contradictions. He quoted Foster (1979:349) to the effect that "all normative group behavior . . . is a function of a particular understanding of the conditions that delimit and determine life" and argued that Foster thus should be regarded as a "cultural idealist" (Harris 1979:298). Foster, however, did not maintain that the "conditions that delimit and determine life" are caused by patterns of thought; instead, he argued that individuals behave in accordance with the understanding of those conditions that they hold as a result of their shared enculturative experiences. Therefore Foster was not a cultural idealist. His position on cultural causality was clear in his statement that the "key factor" influencing change in Tzintzuntzan is to be found in "the village's inherent economic potential, its natural resources, its geographical location, the national and international demand for its present and potential products, and its population growth" (Foster 1979:351). Harris (1979:298) cited this statement as evidence of Foster's inconsistency. Foster's statements would be inconsistent if Foster were a cultural idealist, but Foster was a cultural determinist, and his statements therefore were perfectly consistent. There is nothing inconsistent about asserting, on the one hand, that culture determines behavior, and then affirming, on the other, that material factors determine culture.

"Why then has Foster devoted the entire book to the study of the *image*," Harris (1979:298; emphasis in original) asked, if Foster recognizes that the "key factor" behind sociocultural change lies in material constraints? The answer is simple: because Foster was working with a paradigm that was not concerned with identifying the key factors behind economic development or sociocultural change. Foster admitted that political, economic, and environmental conditions determine economic opportunity, but he did so as an afterthought or an aside. As a cultural determinist, his real concern was with how people perceive and recognize economic opportunity (Foster 1974:55–56). Harris (1980b:374) said that "if opportunities present themselves, some individuals will always take advantage of them, regardless of the image of limited good." Foster would agree. Granted, Foster argued that the image of limited good must be changed before economic development can take place, but he also argued that the image will change when the economic conditions change: "Change cognitive orientation *through changing access to opportunity*, and the peasant will do very well indeed" (Foster 1965:310; emphasis added). Foster 1979:371) offered these comments on the world view of Tzintzuntzenos in 1979: "A Limited Good mentality, although still found among many of the older people, is no longer a significant brake on change, as it certainly was in 1945. Genuine and significant increases in economic and social opportunities, coupled with the villagers' realizations that these opportunities are available to them, underlie these dramatic developments." It is the "villagers' realizations" that Foster wanted to study; the image of limited good was nothing more than a characterization of the typical villagers' realizations between 1945 and 1965.

In the wake of all this brouhaha, Foster (1979:384–385) attempted to defend his concept of the image of limited good in an addendum to his original monograph. In an epilogue to *Tzintzuntzan*, Foster admitted that the image is no longer characteristic of contemporary Tzintzuntzenos, but he maintained that it was a true and accurate description of the world view of Mexican peasants before 1965. What Foster failed to understand was that the debate was never concerned with substantive issues. The controversy surrounding the image of limited good had nothing to do with whether the theory fits the data; it was simply and purely a paradigmatic debate between incommensurable paradigms conducted as though the paradigms had been commensurable.

In sum, the debate about the image of limited good was initiated by cultural materialists who failed to recognize the incommensurability of cultural determinism and perpetuated by cultural determinists who failed to recognize the incommensurability of cultural materialism. The attack was ill-advised; the defense was ill-conceived; and the entire episode was a hindrance to a discipline that would be a science. Ironically, the paradigm of cultural determinism is highly vulnerable to attack, if cultural materialists and others only would evaluate cultural determinism on its own terms. Foster's explanations had very little predictive power. The image of limited good was simply an economical description of the world view of peasants; in effect, Foster explained that peasants viewed the world the way they did because they viewed the world the way they did. Cultural determinists and cultural materialists currently are involved in another debate that is even more imprecise, more vitriolic, and more damaging to the discipline. It is a debate initiated this time by cultural determinists, and it concerns the sacred cow of India.

Suggestions for Further Reading

The concept of the image of limited good finds its fullest expression in George Foster's (1979) *Tzintzuntzan;* for a critique of the model, see Acheson (1972) and Harris (1979).

16

The Intractable
Sacred Cow

The sacred cow controversy began more than twenty years ago and presently shows few signs of abating (see Lodrick 1984; Westen 1984; Murray 1986). Anthropologists, geographers, economists, agronomists, ecologists, psychologists, veterinarians, Indian specialists, government officials, and many others all have joined in the debate—conducted, for the most part, in the pages of *Current Anthropology*—but the basic issues remain unresolved and are, if anything, even more muddled than they were at the outset of the controversy. These facts alone should make it clear that the sacred cow controversy is not a substantive debate. If data alone could resolve the issue, the controversy would have died out long ago. The sacred cow controversy will remain alive as long as there are cultural determinists and cultural materialists who fail to understand the notion of paradigmatic incommensurability.

I want to review the essential outline of the controversy as it has developed during the past two decades since the publication of Harris's (1965) original argument for the adaptive utility of India's sacred cow complex. I think I can demonstrate that the controversy is centered upon a paradigmatic clash between cultural determinism and cultural materialism. Although most of the arguments offered in the debate can be characterized as either cultural deterministic or cultural materialistic, there obviously are other paradigms involved. Chief among these other paradigms is dialectical materialism, which surfaces in the sacred cow controversy in the contributions of Diener (1979; 1980; 1981); Diener, Nonini, and Robkin (1978); Nonini (1980; 1981; 1982); and Robkin (1979; 1981; 1982). The dialectical materialists, however, have made very little impression upon either the cultural determinists or the cultural materialists; in the paradigmatic clash regarding the status of India's cattle, the dialectical materialists have participated in minor skirmishes only. The real battle, with all its noise and commotion, is fought elsewhere. Accordingly, the arguments of the dialectical materialists will be omitted from the following discussion. Robkin's (1979:486) contention that "knowledge [i.e., etic knowledge] that attempts to be 'culture free' would be, by its nature, inhuman and anti-scientific" is characteristic of the dialectical materialist position.

The Sacred Cow Controversy

The sacred cow controversy began in earnest with the appearance of Harris's (1966) article entitled "The Cultural Ecology of India's Sacred Cattle." In that article, Harris (ibid.:50) argued that "the explanation of [beef-eating] taboos . . . [should] be sought in 'positive-functioned' and probably 'adaptive' processes of the ecological system." Noting that the Hindu doctrine of *ahimsa* (nonviolence and respect for all forms of life) had often been cited as an example of the economic irrationality of belief systems, he maintained that humans and bovines in India exist in a symbiotic relationship. According to Harris, the sanctity of India's cattle helps to protect and preserve that relationship. Harris observed that Indian cattle provide small although not insignificant supplies of milk, but that the chief positive contributions provided by the cattle were the fuel and fertilizer obtained from their dung. Harris's analysis was conducted explicitly under the auspices of cultural materialism. He sought to identify the determinants of certain aspects of the Hindu belief system, and he found those determinants in the functional utility of India's cattle.

The initial reaction to Harris's argument was largely favorable. Most reviewers found themselves in essential agreement with Harris, although each had some reservations or qualifications. Suttles (1966:63), for example, was careful to point out that Harris's argument could not be labeled "environmental or economic determinism" because the "doctrine [of the sacred cow] arose, as all do, out of human speculation." That qualification hardly was necessary because Harris's argument presumed that the doctrine was a product of the human imagination (no one has yet suggested that the cattle devised the notion of their own sanctity).

Harris simply wished to show why the human imagination had taken the particular turn it took in India.

The origin of the sacred cow controversy, however, can be found among that same set of initial comments on Harris's article. Andrew Vayda (1966:63) observed that Harris was "at pains to dismiss the influence of ahimsa instead of inquiring whether the doctrine itself has adaptive value." Vayda (ibid.) argued that "it is, at the very least, a reasonable hypothesis that part of the selective process in human evolution is the emergence of beliefs and moral valuations conducive to behavior that helps populations to survive." Yet Vayda's comments were made in reference to an article that clearly argued that the Hindu belief system encouraged and supported behavior that facilitated the survival of the Indian population. Why then did Vayda say what he said?

There are only two possibilities. Either Vayda was disinclined toward scientific discourse, or he was offering his comments in another paradigmatic vein. The second alternative seems overwhelmingly probable, not only for the lack of other evidence to doubt Vayda's integrity, but because his mistake has been repeated by dozens of other scholars with reference to this very issue. Something systematic is going on here, and it poses a serious danger to the science of anthropology.

The only way to make sense of Vayda's comments is to assume that Vayda was speaking from a set of cultural determinist principles. When Vayda said that Harris was at pains to dismiss the influence of *ahimsa*, Vayda only could have meant that Harris was at pains to dismiss the influence of *ahimsa* on individual behavior. Like Foster, who accused Acheson of economic reductionism, Vayda imagined Harris had reduced culture to mere economic variables when it was patently obvious to Vayda that religious sentiment affects the way Indians regard and behave toward their cattle. Thus the debate is between proponents of two incommensurable paradigmatic approaches; one approach wishes to identify the determinants of behavior and the other, the determinants of culture.

In his reply to Vayda, Harris (1966) listed five specific ways in which the Hindu doctrine of *ahimsa* contributed to the positive effectiveness of the Indian cultural ecological system. The damage had been done, however, and cultural determinists to this day persist in insisting that religion does have an influence in India.

In a subsequent issue of *Current Anthropology*, Bennett (1967:251) accused Harris of a "classic functionalist reification." The Indian ecosystem, according to Bennett, does not operate at a peak of efficiency (Harris, incidentally, never claimed that it did), and Bennett devoted the bulk of his critique to a call for a change in the Indian ecosystem; specifically, he wanted to establish a greater market value for the cattle.

Here, then, is yet another incommensurable paradigm, namely, applied anthropology, which, in Bennett's formulation, considers any analysis that fails to promote economic development to be an erroneous analysis. Bennett (ibid.:252) also revealed his cultural determinist bent, however, in maintaining that "religious beliefs . . . cannot be written off completely, no matter what Harris says." Nothing that Harris had written or has written since can reasonably be interpreted as a "writing off" of religious beliefs.

The next major contribution to the sacred cow controversy was made by an economist, Alan Heston. Heston (1971) argued that if the slaughter of cattle were allowed, the Indian cattle population would diminish, the economic output of the remaining cattle would increase, and land would be freed for crop production. Heston's arguments may or may not have merit, although it is difficult to imagine how Indian farmers would benefit from more acreage without the draught animals to plow the land. But these, at least, are empirical claims and can be tested and debated as such. Heston (ibid.:192), however, made other claims in supposed rebuttal to Harris's position: "I also show that the present Indian cattle complex appears to be definitely influenced by the . . . Hindu reverence for the cow." Here Heston compounded the error made by Vayda and Bennett. "If we are willing to follow Harris and ignore the sanctity of the cow," Heston (ibid.:197) argued, we will be doomed to tolerate the inefficiencies of the Indian economic system. Far from ignoring the sanctity of the cow, Harris had been concerned with explaining the reasons for the apotheosis of the cow as well as with identifying the adaptive consequences of the Hindu veneration of cattle.

Bennett (1971:197) agreed with Heston that "Harris's way of presenting his argument is not particularly conducive to . . . dialogue" between anthropologists and other social scientists. Harris's (1966) original presentation included a critique of the conventional wisdom that the sanctity of Indian cattle resulted in exclusively negative economic and ecological effects, but beyond that it is difficult to imagine what Bennett and Heston meant when they said that Harris's style of presentation was not conducive to dialogue. The essence of the scientific method is the persistent critique of arguments. Harris's argument was presented in propositional fashion, and that is all that can be demanded of scientific critiques. Other reviewers, including Hamilton (1971) and Mencher (1971), drew attention to the ways in which Heston had misrepresented Harris's position. Harris (1971) himself reiterated that his position was and always had been that religion does play a part in the Indian cultural ecological system.

The sacred cow controversy intensified following the contribution of a geographer, Frederick Simoons. Simoons (1979:476) echoed the cultural determinists' fear of economic reductionism in his stated intention "to avoid the oversimplification and error that seems inherent in Harris's technoenvironmentalism." According to Simoons (ibid.:475), "It is unfortunate . . . that Harris fails to stress sufficiently the negative impact of the sacred cow concept." Among the negative impacts identified by Simoons were inefficient breeding of cattle and the wasting of available beef. (Harris, of course, never argued that the effects of the sacred cow concept were exclusively positive.) But Simoons (ibid.:473) also concluded that the "analysis of the available data suggests that the numbers, distribution, and composition of India's cattle population are mainly determined not by religion but by geographic and economic factors." That is precisely what Harris had contended in his original article— and, by this time, in two books (Harris 1974; 1977)—yet Simoons offered his statement as a rebuttal to Harris.

Remarkably, several commentators joined Simoons in the chorus against "Harris's technoenvironmentalism." Batra (1979:476), for example, agreed with Simoons "that the sanctity of the cow in India is influenced by the sociopolitical system and that economic materialism is insufficient to explain it." Ferro-Luzzi (1979:478) "wholly" agreed with Simoons "that cattle management in India cannot be explained only in terms of rationality and adaptive utility, as Harris claims." Hoffpauir (1979:482) commented that Simoons had correctly pointed out the weaknesses of Harris's "narrow-minded technoenvironmental determinism." Lodrick (1979:483) faulted Harris for his "reluctance to accept that religious beliefs can influence behavior without some underlying functional rationale." Mishra (1979:484) concluded that "the record is overwhelmingly against Harris's thesis" and argued that the cow "simultaneously belongs to the economic basis and the ideological edifice of the social order" (ibid.:485). Assuming that that last statement has any propositional content, who did—or would—ever argue otherwise?

For paradigmatic confusion, however, no comment on Simoons' article rivaled that of S. L. Malik.

> The basic assumption in the hypothesis of both Harris and Simoons— that the cow in India is merely an economic entity—falls short of reality. Systematic analysis of the concept of the sacred cow in India would have provided evidence that the cow is esteemed in Hindu culture apart from its economic advantages (as delineated by Harris) and/or disadvantages (as shown by Simoons). Whether or not cows should be slaughtered therefore depends not on their economic importance, but on their sacredness (1979:484).

Harris never suggested that the cow is esteemed in India for its economic advantages—the cow is esteemed because the cow is considered sacred. The question Harris addressed was why the cow is considered sacred. Harris's basic assumption was not that the cow is merely an economic entity, but that the sacredness of the cow preserves and protects the cow's economic utility. Malik's contention that the question of whether to slaughter a cow depends upon the sacredness of the cow rather than its economic importance betrays a misunderstanding of paradigmatic issues as well as a misrepresentation of Harris's position. If Malik meant that individual Hindus are consciously motivated by religious beliefs, then he was making a self-evident statement that had nothing whatsoever to do with Harris's analysis. But if Malik meant that sacred cows are not slaughtered because they are sacred, then his statement was not explanatory.

A particularly striking feature of the sacred cow controversy at this stage is the development of a vituperative and strongly personal element in the debate. Commenting upon Simoons' article, Palmieri (1979:485) referred to Harris as "one of the most forceful contenders" in the debate and charged that "Harris has transformed the contest into a . . . crusade for positive-functioned technoenvironmentalism." Schwartzberg (1979:489) remarked that "Harris's horse *ought* to be dead, but he refuses to let it die" (emphasis in original). Noting that Harris "reveals a remarkable unwillingness to learn from others more knowledgeable than himself," Schwartzberg (ibid.) observed that "if anything, Harris's arguments get worse with the passage of time." Simoons (1979:490) charged in a reply to his reviewers that Harris prevents "a dispassionate exchange of ideas" and that "many view the writings of a single investigator, Marvin Harris, as primarily responsible" for keeping the issue clouded and unresolved. One perceptive reviewer, Calvin Schwabe (1979:488), noted the "unnecessarily polemical pedantry of much of the discussion" and wondered if the controversy was about sacred cows or Marvin Harris.

To date, some of the most profound paradigmatic confusion in the sacred cow controversy has been sown not by economists or geographers but by two anthropologists who have conducted ethnographic field research in India: Stanley Freed and Ruth Freed. Freed and Freed (1981) followed Simoons' confusing and misleading article with a befuddling contribution of their own entitled "Sacred Cows and Water Buffalo in India: The Uses of Ethnography." Freed and Freed (ibid.:489) revealed their paradigmatic commitment when they asked, "Why was the hypothesis that religious sentiment is unimportant in affecting behavior ever taken seriously?" As uncritical cultural determinists, Freed and Freed (ibid.:483) were unable to appreciate the import of the cultural materialist argument about India's sacred cattle and consequently failed to critique that argument in an appropriate fashion: "The original and still principal point at issue is whether the composition of the Indian cattle population is determined solely by technoenvironmental factors or whether the Hindu belief in the sacredness of the zebu cow is a significant independent variable."

As Harris (1981a:492) stated in his comments on the Freed and Freed article, "This is false and misleading." The original issue was whether the taboo on the slaughter and consumption of cattle had positive effects for the operation of the Indian cultural ecological system. No one, certainly not Harris, ever had suggested that the composition of the Indian cattle population was determined solely by technoenvironmental factors.

In fact, very few commentators on the debate have correctly perceived Harris's argument. Eric Gans (1985:85) was a notable exception. This was his characterization of Harris's position: "[Marvin Harris's] basic argument is very simple: refuting those who emphasize the irrationality of the Hindu ban on the slaughter of cattle, supposedly the result of an exaggerated respect for arbitrary religious laws, Harris demonstrates that the practice is in fact economically adaptive." Gans was not entirely sympathetic with cultural materialism, but, to his credit, he said he found Harris's defense of his position convincing and was quite correct in noting that Harris's argument was very simple and straightforward. Again, however, Gans was and is one of the few writers on the sacred cow controversy to recognize that fact.

In his comments on the Freed and Freed article, Harris (1981a:492) stated that the authors had completely misunderstood and misrepresented his position. In reply, Freed and Freed (1981:501) declared that "their understanding of Harris's position is in accord with those of other writers on the sacred cow controversy." Regrettably true, but surely Freed and Freed would agree that scientists have an obligation not to compound the errors of their colleagues.

After reading Harris's comments, Freed and Freed still did not understand the extent of their error, but they realized at least that Harris objected to their characterization of his position. They concluded, therefore (1981:501), that the difference must be due to some change in Harris's thinking: "If Harris now believes that the position he has steadfastly maintained for many years is untenable, it behooves him to present the evidence that has caused him to change his mind and accept the influence of religious sentiment on cattle demography."

More than fifteen years after the debate began, Freed and Freed were unaware that the sacred cow controversy is a paradigmatic controversy. They imagined that "evidence" will be sufficient to sway the debate's participants from their original positions. The article by Freed and Freed contained more misrepresentations and misinterpretations than nearly any other contribution to the sacred cow controversy, yet from their paradigmatic perspective, Freed and Freed (ibid.:501) sincerely believed that "Harris has sown a good deal of confusion concerning Indian cattle."

In a telling comment, Freed and Freed (ibid.:489) lamented the "decline in holistic ethnography" and called for the pursuit of intensive ethnographic fieldwork to solve the sacred cow controversy. "More fieldwork" is a characteristic rallying cry of beleaguered cultural determinists. Freed and Freed's "holistic ethnography" is an emotive symbol, not a propositional statement. Predictably, the call for "more fieldwork" strikes a responsive chord among anthropologists, and Freed and Freed were rewarded for having sounded the trumpet. Ballard (1981:490) expressed his appreciation to Freed and Freed for having been reminded that "real-life behavior is always multidimensional and that it is dangerous to attempt any analysis or interpretation in the absence of detailed ethnographic information."

Freed and Freed's cultural determinist interpretation of the sacred cow complex also received support. Ferreira (1981:492) concluded that "the sacredness of the cow is as important in India as technoenvironmental factors." Mishra (1981:495) described Freed and Freed's article as "yet another blow to the cultural symbiotic or techno-environmental doctrine." Fuller (1981:492) wrote that "I have never been able to understand how anyone who had studied in India could seriously hold on to the position that Hindu veneration of the cow has no effect on Hindu's treatment, in the widest sense, of their cattle."

Several months after the appearance of Freed and Freed's article, Srivastava and Malik (1982) suggested that holistic ethnography might not be appropriately applied to the study of complex industrial societies. They argued that the issue at stake in the sacred cow controversy was unimportant, but they understood that issue to be the determination of "whether the significance of cattle is economic or religious" (ibid.:223). In reply, Freed and Freed (1982a) substituted Srivastava and Malik's error with one of their own. The real question, according to Freed and Freed (ibid.:223), is "whether this religious belief affects the way that Hindus manage their cattle." Further, they argued, "the most effective response to the technoenvironmental position is to demonstrate that religion does have an effect upon the management of Indian cattle" (ibid.). The "technoenvironmental position" to which Freed and Freed refer is not, of course, an accurate characterization of the cultural materialist argument; the position is instead the child of an unhappy marriage between two incommensurable paradigms.

The next major installment in the ongoing saga of the sacred cow controversy was an article coauthored by Harris (Vaidyanathan, Nair, and Harris 1982). In that article, the authors attempted to demonstrate that regional variations in the age, sex, and species ratios of Indian bovines (cattle and water buffalo) are determined primarily by demographic, economic, technological, and environmental factors. Vaidyanathan, Nair, and Harris (ibid.:365) were careful to assert that their argument "does not mean that religion has had 'no effect' . . . on the management of India's bovine resources." As a consequence, Freed and Freed (1982b:376) concluded that "Harris [now] appears to have accepted the fact that the Hindu belief in the sanctity of the zebu cow does have an effect upon the management of cattle in India."

As of this writing, the most recent major installment in the debate surrounding Marvin Harris, the sacred cow, and cultural materialism is Westen's (1984) contribution entitled "Cultural Materialism: Food for Thought or Bum Steer?" The logical errors Westen makes in that article have been discussed in Chapter 10; suffice to say that Westen failed to offer either new substantive data regarding the adaptive utility of India's cattle (that was expressly not Westen's purpose) or a novel theoretical approach to the problem. In his comments on Westen's article, Harris (1984) claimed accurately that he had anticipated and dealt with all of Westen's major arguments in previous publications.

Throughout the course of the sacred cow controversy, in fact, Harris consistently has corrected the errors of the cultural determinists each time those errors had been made, and each time his efforts have been to no avail. What Harris has failed to do is to appreciate why his detractors make the errors of interpretation that they make. Harris made the same errors in his analysis of Foster's concept of the image of limited good and did so for the same reasons.

Nevertheless, anthropologists should appreciate the very real contributions that Marvin Harris and other cultural materialists have made to our understanding of the cattle complex in India and to our understanding of food taboos in general (see Harris 1985b). By the same token, anthropologists should appreciate the very real contributions that cultural determinists have made in devising an economical and memorable representation of the world view of peasants. My remarks in these chapters should not be interpreted as a denigration of the research efforts of either cultural materialists or cultural determinists. With respect to the sacred cow controversy, cultural materialists deserve credit for having demonstrated the adaptive utility of the cattle complex, for having identified a plausible scenario for the origin of that complex, and for having explained the reasons for the regional variations in age and sex ratios among India's bovines. With respect to the controversy surrounding the image of limited good, cultural determinists deserve credit for having communicated effectively the peasants' rationale and for having done much to counter U.S. middle-class ethnocentrism about the economic value of thrift, perseverance, and hard work.

What I have tried to demonstrate in these chapters, however, is simply that the debates surrounding India's sacred cow and the world view of peasants have been emotive and ineffective despite (and, partially, because of) the best efforts of cultural materialists and cultural determinists alike. If there is blame to be assigned, it is blame shared by both parties for failing to appreciate the concept of paradigmatic incommensurability. That is not a mistake that anthropologists can afford to make.

The Challenge of Science

If paradigmatic debate in anthropology is to signify anything, anthropologists must learn how to compare and evaluate incommensurable paradigms. The charges and countercharges that abound in the limited good and sacred cow debates make no reference to paradigmatic issues, yet, in these two debates, there are very few substantive points of contention. For the most part, the anthropologists who initiated the debates did so merely for the opportunity to propagandize on behalf of their chosen paradigms. There is a pronounced lack of propositional statements in the controversies. In each case, those who initiated the debates did so without a complete understanding of the position they were attacking; and in each case those who defended their positions did so without reference to the crucial concept of paradigmatic incommensurability. If anthropologists wish to consider themselves members of a scientific community, they must debate issues in a propositional fashion. If the issues in question involve incommensurable paradigmatic approaches, anthropologists must conduct the debate accordingly.

Unfortunately, the style of debate characteristic of the limited good and sacred cow controversies is not uncommon in contemporary anthropology. All too often, anthropologists summarily reject analyses that have been produced under the auspices of paradigms other than their own. Anthropologists have personal and professional investments in particular research strategies and particular patterns of interpretation. The criticisms anthropologists make of rival perspectives often carry a primarily emotive meaning, despite the fact that those criticisms usually are expressed in what would appear to be propositional form. What anthropologists really mean, very often, is that their graduate training was worthwhile, or that the problems they find interesting and meaningful are interesting and meaningful, or that their careers have been significant and productive. I suggest, for example, that Freed and Freed's comments in the sacred cow controversy can be understood in this light.

Cultural determinism and cultural materialism should be compared and evaluated, but the controversies surrounding the image of limited good and the sacred cow of India never should have developed. If there is a significant research problem in the world view of peasants, it concerns the ways in which peasants perceive and interpret the world and the ways in which those perceptions and interpretations influence and determine the personal identities of peasants. As such, it is a problem that could be most profitably investigated by symbolic anthropology. If anthropologists wish to consider the adaptive significance of India's cattle complex, that is a problem that could be addressed most profitably by cultural materialism. Obviously, too, there are aspects of the world view of peasants that could be investigated by cultural materialists (for example, the external determinants of that world view), just as there are aspects of the Indian cattle complex that could be investigated by symbolic anthropologists (for example, the significance of the Hindu veneration of cattle for Indian identity). The initial question to be addressed is whether the research problem at hand concerns the maintenance of human life or the maintenance of human identity. Once that question has been answered, the appropriate paradigm can be brought to bear.

My main goal in closely examining these two debates, however, has not been to establish the "truth" about the image of limited good or the sacred cow, but to examine the nature of these debates. I believe social science in the late twentieth century is facing a crisis of monumental proportions: namely, a crisis of confidence stemming from the fact that so much of what is passed off as social "science" is trivial at best and nonsensical at worse. The unclarity of thought and imprecision of expression evident in the limited good and sacred cow debates are, regrettably, common in contemporary social science.

If anthropologists cannot recognize paradigmatic issues and conduct propositional debates among themselves, how can they expect to meet the challenge of competing paradigms from outside the discipline? Contemporary "scientific" creationists may not pose a very significant intellectual challenge to the genuinely scientific theory of evolution, but the political threat they pose to the legitimacy of anthropological knowledge is very real and very serious. We could do a better job of facing that threat. The crucial distinction between science and pseudoscience is an epistemological one, not a theoretical one. Yet most public debates between anthropologists and creationists have centered on theoretical issues, which is not the proper way to compare incommensurable paradigms.

In the long run, the danger posed by pseudoscience may well be the least of our worries. It is not pseudoscientists, but rather legitimate, recognized social scientists who have defined drug abuse and overeating as diseases; it is social scientists who have combined fortune telling and electronics to produce polygraph tests; and it is social scientists who have supported and sanctioned the logical absurdity of the insanity defense. The most notorious examples of nonpropositional, nonfalsifiable social science, of course, can be found in contemporary Western psychotherapy—but much of contemporary Western psychotherapy is accepted as legitimate science by much of the social scientific community. As scientists, we must condemn the improper use of the scientific method; otherwise we will be guilty by association with those who offer emotive statements disguised as scientific propositions.

In comparison with anthropology, other social sciences are handicapped by their failure to recognize the pervasive significance of culture in human life and by their refusal to maintain a rigorous distinction between emic and etic knowledge. Anthropology enjoys an advantage in that respect, but it is not an advantage that has been sufficient to protect the discipline from sloppy, unscientific thinking or meaningless, nonpropositional debate. It is possible for human beings to study themselves scientifically, and as anthropologists, we have a special obligation to pursue a scientific inquiry into the human condition: first, because ours is the one social science that contains the requisite theoretical and epistemological standards for an adequate investigation of human life, and second, because some of the other social sciences contain too much emotive thinking.

Suggestions for Further Reading

As of this date, the major articles in the ongoing debate over India's sacred cow have been "The Cultural Ecology of India's Sacred Cattle," by Marvin Harris (1966); "On the Cultural Ecology of Indian Cattle," by John Bennett (1967); "An Approach to the Sacred Cow of India," by Alan Heston (1971); "Questions in the Sacred Cow Controversy," by Frederick Simoons (1979); "Sacred Cows and Water Buffalo in India," by Stanley and Ruth Freed (1981); "Bovine Sex and Species Ratios in India," by Vaidyanathan, Nair, and Harris (1982); and "Cultural Materialism: Food for Thought or Bum Steer?" by Drew Westen (1984).

Epilogue

*How has it been possible to believe
in the amorality of life?*
—José Ortega y Gasset,
The Revolt of the Masses

By way of brief summary, I have attempted to establish four basic points
in the four parts of this book: first, that science alone among the various
ways of obtaining knowledge about the empirical world consistently
appeals to responsible epistemological foundations; second, that anthropology has a uniquely valuable set of ontological, epistemological,
and theoretical assumptions for the study of the human condition; third,
that the complementary paradigms of cultural materialism and symbolic
anthropology constitute the best research strategies available to contemporary anthropologists for the analysis of the human experience;
and fourth, that the inherent dangers of nonpropositional debate threaten
to undermine the scientific utility of the discipline.

In the final analysis, however, I have attempted to make but one
essential point—namely, that knowledge about the human condition can
be sought either responsibly or irresponsibly. As scientists, anthropologists have a responsibility to formulate empirically falsifiable accounts,
descriptions, and analyses of the human condition. As citizens, anthropologists have a responsibility to consider the social and moral
implications of their conclusions about human behavior. Other social
scientists share these same responsibilities. But the obligation to seek
knowledge about the human condition in a responsible manner is not
restricted to those who make their careers explaining human life.

Everyone everywhere wants to understand human life, and everyone
everywhere makes some attempt to do so. The sad conclusion of

153

anthropological research is that nearly everyone does so unscientifically. People everywhere are content with simplistic answers; people everywhere hold inconsistent beliefs; people everywhere regard emotive utterances as propositional statements; people everywhere embrace the knowledge obtained by faith and revelation, even though their daily lives provide abundant evidence to disconfirm their beliefs. Human beings are meaning-seeking animals, but cross-culturally and panhistorically, epistemological responsibility is a rarity.

The key to epistemological responsibility, in my view, is an uncompromising commitment to propositional knowledge, and that is the point I have tried to stress throughout this book. The way to guard against prejudice, bigotry, shortsightedness, and rationalization—in our own lives and in the pursuit of science—is to ensure that our understandings of the world accord reliably and consistently with the reality of the world. To do that, we must ensure that our scientific theories are falsifiable. If we do not do so, then our theories are more likely than not to be self-serving, and we sacrifice not only our self-respect but our trustworthiness as well.

The dangers posed by epistemological irresponsibility are not simply academic or intellectual. Ethos and world view are interdependent; we can only decide what ought to be the case if we truly know what is the case. An unreliable world view makes an unstable foundation for a defensible ethos. Without some shared ontological assumptions—without some common point of reference—there can be no morality. All "moral" issues are actually epistemological debates. The contemporary controversy about abortion, for example, can be posed first as an ontological question—"What is a human being?"—and then as an epistemological one—"How can we know?" What we know about the world depends upon how we know it.

In this book, I have been concerned explicitly with the challenge of theory, or, as I have called it in other contexts, the challenge of epistemology, the challenge of philosophy, or the challenge of science. All of these, in the end, are simply aspects of the challenge of life. To my mind, the most responsible and productive social scientists are those who are reflective, discriminating, and skeptical. Life may be an insoluble puzzle, but if we are to make any claims to dignity, nobility, courage, or integrity, we must make a responsible attempt to solve that puzzle. I hold the unstartling and unoriginal yet profound conviction that human beings are responsible for their actions, and I hold much of contemporary social science responsible for having suggested otherwise.

These are personal convictions, which I readily admit. I am convinced that there is an inescapable link between the conclusions I have reached in this book about the proper conduct of science and the values I have expressed in these last paragraphs about the moral dimensions of epistemology—however, I realize that not everyone will agree with me. I mention my position in the hope of inspiring critical reflection on these issues. In the end, we are all faced with the same challenges. My point ultimately is that the anthropological enterprise is neither irrelevant nor inconsequential; it is, instead, ineluctably part of the human enterprise.

One final word. The anthropological approach is not the be all and end all of responsible inquiry. Anthropology is not the key to the puzzle of life, and I would not want to be understood as having suggested that it was. My concern in this book simply has been to demonstrate that the anthropological approach is a uniquely and exceptionally valuable approach to understanding important dimensions of human life. Nevertheless, although sound anthropological investigation may be a sufficient condition for insight into the human condition, it is hardly a necessary condition. Science is progressive; even the best anthropological descriptions and analyses are likely to be supplanted eventually by more incisive accounts. For that reason, I suspect that good philosophy and good literature will last far longer than good anthropology—although I also think that a world without good anthropology would be an impoverished world.

Bibliography

Abel, Reuben, 1976. *Man Is the Measure.* New York: Free Press.

Aceves, Joseph B., and H. Gill King, 1979. *Introduction to Anthropology.* Morristown, N.J.: General Learning Press.

Acheson, James M., 1972. "Limited Good or Limited Goods? Response to Economic Opportunity in a Tarascan Pueblo." *American Anthropologist* 74:1152–1169.

_____ . 1974. "Reply to George Foster." *American Anthropologist* 76:57–62.

Arendt, Hannah, 1958. *The Human Condition.* Chicago: University of Chicago Press.

Arensberg, Conrad M., 1972. "Culture as Behavior: Structure and Emergence." *Annual Review of Anthropology* 1:1–26.

Ballard, Roger, 1981. "Comment on: 'Sacred Cows and Water Buffalo in India,' by S. A. Freed and Ruth S. Freed." *Current Anthropology* 22:490.

Barnett, Homer G., 1953. *Innovation: The Basis of Cultural Change.* New York: McGraw-Hill.

Barnouw, Victor, 1985. *Culture and Personality.* 4th ed. Homewood, Ill.: Dorsey Press.

Barrett, Stanley R., 1984. *The Rebirth of Anthropological Theory.* Toronto: University of Toronto Press.

Batra, S. M., 1979. "Comment on: 'Questions in the Sacred-Cow Controversy,' by F. J. Simoons." *Current Anthropology* 20:476.

Bee, Robert L., 1974. *Patterns and Processes: An Introduction to Anthropological Strategies for the Study of Sociocultural Change.* New York: Free Press.

Benedict, Ruth, 1934. *Patterns of Culture.* Boston: Houghton Mifflin.

Bennett, John W., 1967. "On the Cultural Ecology of Indian Cattle." *Current Anthropology* 8:251–252.

_____ . 1971. "Comment on: 'An Approach to the Sacred Cow of India,' by Alan Heston." *Current Anthropology* 12:197–198.

Binford, Lewis R., 1962. "Archaeology as Anthropology." *American Antiquity* 28:217–225.

_____ . 1968a. "Archeological Perspectives." In *New Perspectives in Archeology.* Sally R. Binford and Lewis R. Binford, eds., pp. 5–32. Chicago: Aldine Publishing.

————. 1968b. "Post-Pleistocene Adaptations." In *New Perspectives in Ar-cheology*. Sally R. Binford and Lewis R. Binford, eds., pp. 313–342. Chicago: Aldine Publishing.

Binford, Lewis, and Jeremy Sabloff, 1982. "Paradigms, Systematics, and Ar-chaeology." *Journal of Anthropological Research* 38:137–153.

Boas, Franz, 1963. *The Mind of Primitive Man*. New York: Free Press (originally published 1911).

Bohannan, Paul, and Mark Glazer, eds., 1973. *High Points in Anthropology*. New York: Alfred A. Knopf.

Broce, Gerald, 1973. *History of Anthropology*. Minneapolis: Burgess Publishing.

Burling, Robbins, 1964. "Cognition and Componential Analysis: God's Truth or Hocus-Pocus?" *American Anthropologist* 66:20–28.

————. 1969. "Linguistics and Ethnographic Description." *American Anthro-pologist* 77:817–827.

Campbell, Donald T., and Raoul Naroll, 1972. "The Mutual Methodological Relevance of Anthropology and Psychology." In *Psychological Anthropology*. Francis L.K. Hsu, ed., pp. 435–463. Cambridge, Mass.: Schenkman Publishing.

Cannon, Walter B., 1942. "'Voodoo' Death." *American Anthropologist* 44:169–181.

Carneiro, Robert L., 1967. "On the Relationships Between Size of Population and Complexity of Social Organization." *Southwestern Journal of Anthropology* 23:234–243.

Chapple, Eliot D., and Conrad M. Arensberg, 1940. "Measuring Human Relations: An Introduction to the Study of the Interaction of Individuals." *Genetic Psychology Monographs* 22:3–147.

Chisholm, Roderick M., 1977. *Theory of Knowledge*. 2nd ed. Englewood Cliffs, N.J.: Prentice-Hall.

Cohen, Ronald, 1970. "Generalizations in Ethnology." In *A Handbook of Method in Cultural Anthropology*. Raoul Naroll and Ronald Cohen, eds., pp. 31–50. New York: Columbia University Press.

Conklin, Harold C., 1955. "Hanunoo Color Categories." *Southwestern Journal of Anthropology* 11:339–344.

————. 1969. "Lexicographical Treatment of Folk Taxonomies." In *Cognitive Anthropology*. Stephen A. Tyler, ed., pp. 41–59. New York: Holt, Rinehart and Winston.

Cornman, James W., and Keith Lehrer, 1968. *Philosophical Problems and Arguments: An Introduction*. New York: Macmillan.

Cunningham, Frank, 1973. *Objectivity in Social Science*. Toronto: University of Toronto Press.

Diamond, Stanley, 1974. "The Myth of Structuralism." In *The Unconscious in Culture: The Structuralism of Claude Levi-Strauss*. Ino Rossi, ed., pp. 292–335. New York: Dutton.

Diener, Paul, 1979. "Comment on: 'Questions in the Sacred Cow Controversy,' by F. J. Simoons." *Current Anthropology* 20:477–478.

————. 1980. "Quantum Adjustment, Macroevolution, and the Social Field: Some Comments on Evolution and Culture." *Current Anthropology* 21:423–443.

_____. 1981. "Comment on: 'Sacred Cows and Water Buffalo in India,' by S. A. Freed and R. S. Freed." *Current Anthropology* 22:491.

Diener, Paul, Donald Nonini, and Eugene E. Robkin, 1978. "The Dialectics of the Sacred Cow: Ecological Adaptation Versus Political Appropriation in the Origins of India's Cattle Complex." *Dialectical Anthropology* 3:221–241.

Dimen-Schein, Muriel, 1977. *The Anthropological Imagination.* New York: McGraw-Hill.

Dolgin, Janet L., David S. Kemnitzer, and David M. Schneider, 1977. "'As People Express Their Lives, So They Are . . . .'" In *Symbolic Anthropology.* Janet L. Dolgin, David S. Kemnitzer, and David M. Schneider, eds., pp. 3–44. New York: Columbia University Press.

Douglas, Jack, ed., 1970. *Understanding Everyday Life: Toward the Reconstruction of Sociological Knowledge.* Chicago: Aldine Publishing.

Durbin, Mridula A., 1972. "Linguistic Models in Anthropology." *Annual Review of Anthropology* 1:383–410.

Edgerton, Robert B., 1969. "On the 'Recognition' of Mental Illness." In *Changing Perspectives in Mental Illness.* Stanley C. Plog and Robert B. Edgerton, eds., pp. 49–72. New York: Holt, Rinehart and Winston.

Ehrenreich, Jeffrey, 1984. "Comment on: 'Cultural Materialism: Food for Thought or Bum Steer?' by Drew Westen." *Current Anthropology* 25 (5):647–648.

Eiseley, Loren, 1946. *The Immense Journey.* New York: Random House.

Erikson, Erik H., 1959. *Identity and the Life Cycle.* New York: International Universities Press.

Feibleman, James K., 1975. *The Stages of Human Life: A Biography of Entire Man.* The Hague: Martinus Nijhoff.

Ferreira, J. V., 1981. "Comment on: 'Sacred Cows and Water Buffalo in India,' by S. A. Freed and Ruth S. Freed." *Current Anthropology* 23:492.

Ferro-Luzzi, Gabriella Eichinger, 1979. "Comment on: 'Questions in the Sacred Cow Controversy,' by F. J. Simoons." *Current Anthropology* 20:478–479.

Feyerabend, Paul, 1975. *Against Method.* Atlantic Highlands, N.J.: Humanities Press.

Flannery, Kent, 1968. "Archeological Systems Theory and Early Mesoamerica." In *Anthropological Archeology in the Americas.* Betty J. Meggers, ed., pp. 67–87. Brooklyn, N.Y.: Theo. Gaus' Sons.

_____. 1982. "The Golden Marshalltown: A Parable for the Archeology of the 1980's." *American Anthropologist* 84:265–278.

Foster, George M., 1965. "Peasant Society and the Image of Limited Good." *American Anthropologist* 67:293–315.

_____. 1974. "Limited Good or Limited Goods: Observations on Acheson." *American Anthropologist* 76:53–57.

_____. 1979. *Tzintzuntzan: Mexican Peasants in a Changing World.* Rev. ed. Boston: Little, Brown (originally published 1967).

Frake, Charles O., 1964a. "A Structural Description of Subanun 'Religious Behavior.'" In *Explorations in Cultural Anthropology.* Ward H. Goodenough, ed., pp. 111–129. New York: McGraw-Hill.

_____. 1964b. "Notes on Queries in Ethnography." *American Anthropologist,* 66 (3):132–145.

————. 1969. "The Ethnographic Study of Cognitive Systems." In *Cognitive Anthropology*. Stephen A. Tyler, ed., pp. 28–41. New York: Holt, Rinehart and Winston.

Frankel, Charles, 1955. *The Case for Modern Man*. New York: Harper.

————. 1960. "Philosophy and the Social Sciences." In *Both Human and Humane: The Humanities and Social Sciences in Graduate Education*. Charles E. Boewe and Roy F. Nichols, eds., pp. 94–117. Philadelphia: University of Pennsylvania Press.

Freed, Stanley S., and Ruth S. Freed, 1981. "Sacred Cows and Water Buffalo in India: The Uses of Ethnography." *Current Anthropology* 22:483–502.

————. 1982a. "Reply to: 'On Ethnography and the Sacred Cow Controversy,' by Vinay Srivastava and S. L. Malik." *Current Anthropology* 23:223.

————. 1982b. "Comment on: 'Bovine Sex and Species Ratios in India,' by A. Vaidyanathan et al." *Current Anthropology* 23:376.

Fuller, S. J., 1981. "Comment on: 'Sacred Cows and Water Buffalo in India,' by S. A. Freed and Ruth S. Freed." *Current Anthropology* 22:492.

Gamst, Frederick C., 1980. "Rethinking Leach's Structural Analysis of Color and Instructional Categories in Traffic Control Signals." In *Beyond the Myths of Culture*. Eric Ross, ed., pp. 359–390. New York: Academic Press.

Gans, Eric, 1985. *The End of Culture: Toward a Generative Anthropology*. Berkeley: University of California Press.

Garbarino, Merwyn S., 1977. *Sociocultural Theory in Anthropology*. New York: Holt, Rinehart and Winston.

Geertz, Clifford, 1973. *The Interpretation of Cultures*. New York: Basic Books.

————. 1977. "From the Native's Point of View: On the Nature of Anthropological Understanding." In *Symbolic Anthropology*. Janet L. Dolgin, David S. Kemnitzer, and David M. Schneider, eds., pp. 480–492. New York: Columbia University Press.

————. 1983. *Local Knowledge: Further Essays in Interpretive Anthropology*. New York: Basic Books.

————. 1986. "Making Experience, Authoring Selves." In *The Anthropology of Experience*. Victor W. Turner and Edward M. Bruner, eds., pp. 373–380. Urbana: University of Illinois Press.

Godelier, Maurice, 1977. *Perspectives in Marxist Anthropology*. New York: Cambridge University Press.

Goffman, Erving, 1961. *Asylums*. Chicago: Aldine Publishing.

Goldenweiser, Alexander A., 1936. "Loose Ends of Theory on the Individual, Pattern, and Involution in Primitive Society." In *Essays in Anthropology Presented to A. L. Kroeber in Celebration of His Sixtieth Birthday, June 11, 1936*, pp. 99–104. Freeport, N.Y.: Books for Libraries Press.

Goldschmidt, Walter, 1983. "Review of *Beyond the Myths of Culture: Essays in Cultural Materialism*." *American Anthropologist* 85:695–698.

Goodenough, Ward H., 1956. "Componential Analysis and the Study of Meaning." *Language* 32:195–216.

————. 1964. "Introduction." In *Explorations in Anthropology*. Ward H. Goodenough, ed., pp. 1–24. New York: McGraw-Hill.

————. 1970. *Description and Comparison in Cultural Anthropology*. Chicago: Aldine Publishing.

Gould, Roger L., 1978. *Transformations: Growth and Change in Adult Life*. New York: Simon and Schuster.

Graburn, Nelson, ed., 1971. *Readings in Kinship and Social Structure*. New York: Harper and Row.

Graebner, Fritz, 1911. *Method of Ethnology* (in German). Heidelberg: Carl Winter's Universitats Buchhandlung.

Hall, Edward T., 1966. *The Hidden Dimension*. Garden City, N.Y.: Doubleday.

Hamilton, James W., 1971. "Comment on: 'An Approach to the Sacred Cow of India,' by Alan Heston." *Current Anthropology* 12:198–199.

Harris, Marvin, 1964. *The Nature of Cultural Things*. New York: Random House.

————. 1965. "The Myth of the Sacred Cow." In *Man, Culture, and Animals*. A. P. Vayda and A. Leeds, eds., pp. 217–228. Washington, D.C.: American Association for the Advancement of Science.

————. 1966. "The Cultural Ecology of India's Sacred Cattle." *Current Anthropology* 7:51–66.

————. 1968. *The Rise of Anthropological Theory*. New York: T. Y. Crowell.

————. 1971. "Comment on: 'An Approach to the Sacred Cow of India,' by Alan Heston." *Current Anthropology* 12:199–201.

————. 1974. *Cows, Pigs, Wars and Witches: The Riddles of Culture*. New York: Random House.

————. 1975. "Why a Perfect Knowledge of All the Rules That One Must Know in Order to Act Like a Native Cannot Lead to a Knowledge of How Natives Act." *Journal of Anthropological Research* 30:242–251.

————. 1976. "History and Significance of the Emic/Etic Distinction." *Annual Review of Anthropology* 5:329–350.

————. 1977. *Cannibals and Kings: The Origins of Cultures*. New York: Random House.

————. 1979. *Cultural Materialism: The Struggle for a Science of Culture*. New York: Random House.

————. 1980. "History and Ideological Significance of the Separation of Social and Cultural Anthropology." In *Beyond the Myths of Culture*. Eric Ross, ed., pp. 391–407. New York: Academic Press.

————. 1981a. "Comment on: 'Sacred Cows and Water Buffalo in India,' by S. A. Freed and R. S. Freed." *Current Anthropology* 22:492–494.

————. 1981b. *America Now: The Anthropology of a Changing Culture*. New York: Simon and Schuster.

————. 1982. "Reply to Paul J. Magnarella." *American Anthropologist* 84:142–145.

————. 1984. "Comment on: 'Cultural Materialism: Food for Thought or Bum Steer?' by Drew Weston." *Current Anthropology*, 25 (5):648–649.

————. 1985a. *Culture, People, Nature: An Introduction to General Anthropology*. 4th ed. New York: Harper and Row.

————. 1985b. *Good to Eat: Riddles of Food and Culture*. New York: Simon and Schuster.

Hatch, Elvin, 1973. *Theories of Man and Culture*. New York: Columbia University Press.

———. 1983. *Culture and Morality: The Relativity of Values in Anthropology*. New York: Columbia University Press.

Hempel, Carl G., 1965. *Aspects of Scientific Explanation and Other Essays in the Philosophy of Science*. New York: Free Press.

Heston, Alan, 1971. "An Approach to the Sacred Cow of India." *Current Anthropology* 12:191–209.

Hodder, Ian, 1982. *Symbolic and Structural Archaeology*. Cambridge: Cambridge University Press.

Hoffpauir, Robert, 1979. "Comment on: 'Questions in the Sacred Cow Controversy,' by F. J. Simoons." *Current Anthropology* 20:482–483.

Hollis, Martin, and Steven Lukes, eds., 1982. *Rationality and Relativism*. Cambridge, Mass.: MIT Press.

Honigmann, John J., 1976. *The Development of Anthropological Ideas*. Homewood, Ill.: Dorsey Press.

Hospers, John, 1967. *An Introduction to Philosophical Analysis*. 2nd ed. Englewood Cliffs, N.J.: Prentice-Hall.

———. 1968. "On Explanation." In *Theory in Anthropology*. Robert A. Manners and David Kaplan, eds., pp. 68–79. Chicago: Aldine Publishing.

Huizinga, Johan, 1950. *Homo Ludens: A Study of the Play Element in Culture*. Boston: Beacon Press.

Hultsch, David F., and Francine Deutsch, 1981. *Adult Development and Aging: A Life-Span Perspective*. New York: McGraw-Hill.

Hunter, David E., and Phillip Whitten, 1976. *Encyclopedia of Anthropology*. New York: Harper and Row.

Jarvie, I. C., 1964. *The Revolution in Anthropology*. New York: Humanities Press.

———. 1984. *Rationality and Relativism: In Search of a Philosophy and History of Anthropology*. Boston: Routledge and Kegan Paul.

Jenkins, Alan, 1979. *The Social Theory of Claude Levi-Strauss*. New York: St. Martin's Press.

Kaplan, David, and Robert A. Manners, 1972. *Culture Theory*. Englewood Cliffs, N.J.: Prentice-Hall.

Keesing, Roger M., 1974. "Theories of Culture." *Annual Review of Anthropology* 3:73–98.

———. 1975. *Kin Groups and Social Structure*. New York: Holt, Rinehart and Winston.

———. 1981. *Cultural Anthropology: A Contemporary Perspective*. 2nd ed. New York: Holt, Rinehart and Winston.

Kennedy, John G., 1973. "Cultural Psychiatry." In *Handbook of Social and Cultural Anthropology*. John J. Honigmann, ed., pp. 1119–1198. Chicago: Rand McNally.

Klemke, E. D., Robert Hollinger, and A. David Kline, eds., 1980. *Introductory Readings in the Philosophy of Science*. Buffalo, N.Y.: Prometheus Books.

Kottak, Conrad Philip, 1987. *Cultural Anthropology*. 4th ed. New York: Random House.

Kroeber, Alfred L., 1939. *Cultural and Native Areas of North America*. University of California Publications in American Archaeology and Ethnology 38:1–242.

Kroeber, Alfred L., and Clyde Kluckhohn, 1963. *Culture: A Critical Review of Concepts and Definitions.* New York: Vintage Books (originally published 1952).

Kuhn, Thomas, 1970a. *The Structure of Scientific Revolutions.* 2nd ed. Chicago: University of Chicago Press.

_____. 1970b. "Logic of Discovery or Psychology of Research?" and "Reflections on My Critics." In *Criticism and the Growth of Knowledge.* Imre Lakatos and Alan Musgrave, eds., pp. 1–25, 231–278. Aberdeen: Cambridge University Press.

_____. 1977. "Second Thoughts on Paradigms." In *The Structure of Scientific Theories.* 2nd ed. Frederick Suppe, ed., pp. 459–481. Urbana: University of Illinois Press.

Kurzweil, Edith, 1980. *The Age of Structuralism.* New York: Columbia University Press.

Lakatos, Imre, 1970. "Falsification and the Methodology of Scientific Research Programmes." In *Criticism and the Growth of Knowledge.* Imre Lakatos and Alan Musgrave, eds., pp. 91–196. Aberdeen: Cambridge University Press.

Lakatos, Imre, and Alan Musgrave, eds., 1970. *Criticism and the Growth of Knowledge.* Cambridge: Cambridge University Press.

Landy, David, ed., 1977. *Culture, Disease, and Healing: Studies in Medical Anthropology.* New York: Macmillan.

Laudan, Larry, 1977. *Progress and Its Problems: Toward a Theory of Scientific Growth.* Berkeley: University of California Press.

Lawless, Robert, 1979. *The Concept of Culture: An Introduction to the Social Sciences.* Minneapolis: Burgess Publishing.

Lawless, Robert, Vinson H. Sutlive, and Mario D. Zamora, eds., 1983. *Fieldwork: The Human Experience.* New York: Gordon and Breach.

Leach, Edmund, 1970. *Levi-Strauss.* London: Wm. Collins.

Lee, Richard, and Irwin DeVore, eds., 1968. *Man the Hunter.* Chicago: Aldine Publishing.

_____. 1977. *Kalahari Hunter-Gatherers: Studies of the !Kung San and Their Neighbors.* Cambridge, Mass.: Harvard University Press.

Leighton, Alexander H., 1969. "A Comparative Study of Psychiatric Disorder in Nigeria and Rural North America." In *Changing Perspectives in Mental Illness.* Stanley C. Plog and Robert B. Edgerton, eds., pp. 179–199. New York: Holt, Rinehart and Winston.

Lett, James, 1981. "Crime and Punishment in a Virgin Island Community." *The Florida Journal of Anthropology* 6:41–51.

_____. 1982. "The British Virgin Islands Tourism Industry: Problems and Prospects for the 1980s." Paper presented at the Seventh Annual Meeting of the Caribbean Studies Association, Kingston, Jamaica, May 26–30.

_____. 1983. "Ludic and Liminoid Aspects of Charter Yacht Tourism in the Caribbean." *Annals of Tourism Research* 10:53–74.

_____. 1985a. "Playground in the Sun." *Chartering,* 2 (4):YV22–23.

_____. 1985b. "More on Media Anthropology." *Anthropology Newsletter,* 26 (3):2.

_____. 1986. "Anthropology and Journalism." *Communicator,* 40 (5):33–35.

————. 1987a. "An Anthropologist on the Anchor Desk." *Practicing Anthropology,* 9 (1):2, 22.

————. 1987b. "An Anthropological View of Television Journalism." *Human Organization* (forthcoming).

Levi-Strauss, Claude, 1963. *Structural Anthropology, Vol. 1.* New York: Basic Books.

————. 1966. *The Savage Mind.* Chicago: University of Chicago Press.

————. 1969a. *The Elementary Structures of Kinship.* Boston: Beacon Press.

————. 1969b. *The Raw and the Cooked.* New York: Harper and Row.

————. 1976. *Structural Anthropology, Vol. 2.* New York: Basic Books.

Lex, Barbara W., 1974. "Voodoo Death: New Thoughts on an Old Explanation." *American Anthropologist* 76:818–823.

Lodrick, Deryck, 1979. "Comment on: 'Questions in the Sacred Cow Controversy,' by F. J. Simoons." *Current Anthropology* 20:483.

————. 1984. "A Cattle Fair in Rajasthan: The Kharwa *Mela.*" *Current Anthropology* 25:218–225.

London, Perry, 1969. "Morals and Mental Health." In *Changing Perspectives in Mental Illness.* Stanley C. Plog and Robert B. Edgerton, eds., pp. 32–48. New York: Holt, Rinehart and Winston.

Lowie, Robert H., 1937. *The History of Ethnological Theory.* New York: Reinhart.

Magnarella, Paul, 1982. "Cultural Materialism and the Problem of Probabilities." *American Anthropologist* 84:138–142.

Malefijt, Annemarie de Waal, 1974. *Images of Man: A History of Anthropological Thought.* New York: Alfred A. Knopf.

Malik, S. L., 1979. "Comment on: 'Questions in the Sacred Cow Controversy,' by F. J. Simoons." *Current Anthropology* 20:484.

Malinowski, Bronislaw, 1922. *Argonauts of the Western Pacific.* London: Routledge.

Manners, Robert A., and David Kaplan, 1968. "Notes on Theory and Non-Theory in Anthropology." In *Theory in Anthropology.* Robert A. Manners and David Kaplan, eds., pp. 1–12. Chicago: Aldine Publishing.

Marx, Karl, and Frederick Engels, 1948. *The Communist Manifesto.* New York: International Publishers (originally published 1848).

Mead, Margaret, 1928. *Coming of Age in Samoa.* New York: William Morrow.

————. 1971. "Comment on: 'An Approach to the Sacred Cow of India,' by Allan Heston." *Current Anthropology* 12:202–204.

Mencher, Joan, 1971. "Comment on: 'The Cultural Ecology of India's Sacred Cattle,' by Marvin Harris." *Current Anthropology* 7:61.

Mishra, S. N., 1979. "Comment on: 'Questions in the Sacred Cow Controversy,' by F. J. Simoons." *Current Anthropology* 20:484–485.

————. 1981. "Comment on: 'Sacred Cows and Water Buffalo in India,' by S. A. Freed and R. S. Freed." *Current Anthropology* 22:495–496.

Morgan, Lewis Henry, 1877: *Ancient Society.* New York: World Publishing.

Murdock, George Peter, 1949. *Social Structure.* New York: Macmillan.

Murphy, Robert, 1980. *The Dialectics of Social Life: Alarms and Excursions in Anthropological Theory.* New York: Columbia University Press (Morningside edition).

Murray, D. W., 1986. "On Keralan Cattle: A Response to Westen and Harris." *Current Anthropology,* 27 (1):53.

Nagel, Ernest, 1961. *The Structure of Science.* New York: Harcourt, Brace and World.

Naroll, Raoul, 1970. "Epistemology." In *A Handbook of Method in Cultural Anthropology.* Raoul Naroll and Ronald Cohen, eds., pp. 25–30. New York: Columbia University Press.

————. 1973. "Introduction." In *Main Currents in Cultural Anthropology.* Raoul Naroll and Frada Naroll, eds., pp. 1–23. Englewood Cliffs, N.J.: Prentice-Hall.

Naroll, Raoul, and Ronald Cohen, eds., 1970. *A Handbook of Method in Cultural Anthropology.* New York: Columbia University Press.

Naroll, Raoul, and Frada Naroll, eds., 1973. *Main Currents in Cultural Anthropology.* Englewood Cliffs, N.J.: Prentice-Hall.

Nonini, Donald M., 1980. "Comment on: 'Quantum Adjustment, Macroevolution, and the Social Field: Some Comments on Evolution and Culture,' by Paul Diener." *Current Anthropology* 21:433–435.

————. 1981. "Comment on: 'Sacred Cows and Water Buffalo in India,' by S. A. Freed and R. S. Freed." *Current Anthropology* 22:496–497.

————. 1982. "Comment on: 'Bovine Sex and Species Ratios in India,' by A. Vaidyanathan et al." *Current Anthropology* 23:377–378.

Oliver, Chad, 1981. *The Discovery of Humanity: An Introduction to Anthropology.* New York: Harper and Row.

Palmieri, Richard P., 1979. "Comment on: 'Questions in the Sacred Cow Controversy,' by F. J. Simoons." *Current Anthropology* 20:485–486.

Parker, Richard, 1985. "From Symbolism to Interpretation: Reflections on the Work of Clifford Geertz." *Anthropology and Humanism Quarterly,* 10 (3):62–67.

Parsons, Talcott, 1937. *The Structure of Social Action.* New York: McGraw-Hill.

Pelto, Pertti J., and Gretel H. Pelto, 1978. *Anthropological Research: The Structure of Inquiry.* 2nd ed. New York: Cambridge University Press.

Pike, Kenneth L., 1967. *Language in Relation to a Unified Theory of the Structures of Human Behavior.* 2nd ed. The Hague: Mouton (originally published 1954).

Polanyi, Michael, 1962. *Personal Knowledge: Towards a Post-Critical Philosophy.* Chicago: University of Chicago Press.

————. 1966. *The Tacit Dimension.* Garden City, N.Y.: Doubleday.

Popper, Karl R., 1959. *The Logic of Scientific Discovery.* London: Hutchinson.

————. 1963. *Conjectures and Refutations: The Growth of Scientific Knowledge.* New York: Basic Books.

————. 1970. "Normal Science and Its Dangers." In *Criticism and the Growth of Knowledge.* Imre Lakatos and Alan Musgrave, eds., pp. 51–58. Aberdeen: Cambridge University Press.

Price, Barbara J., 1982. "Cultural Materialism: A Theoretical Review." *American Antiquity* 47:709–741.

Radcliffe-Brown, A. R., 1952. *Structure and Function in Primitive Society.* London: Cohen and West.

Rappaport, Roy A., 1967. "Ritual Regulation of Environmental Relations Among a New Guinea People." *Ethnology* 6:17–30.

Redman, Charles L., ed., 1973. *Research and Theory in Current Archeology.* New York: John Wiley.

Renfrew, Colin, Michael J. Rowlands, and Barbara Abbott Segraves, eds., 1982. *Theory and Explanation in Archaeology.* New York: Academic Press.

Renner, Egon, 1984. "On Geertz's Interpretive Theoretical Program." *Current Anthropology,* 25 (4):538–540.

Rice, Kenneth A., 1980. *Geertz and Culture.* Ann Arbor: University of Michigan Press.

Richardson, Miles, 1984. "Comment on: 'The Thick and the Thin: On the Interpretive Program of Clifford Geertz,' by Paul Shankman." *Current Anthropology,* 25 (3):275.

Robkin, Eugene R., 1979. "Comment on: 'Questions in the Sacred Cow Controversy,' by F. J. Simoons." *Current Anthropology* 20:486–488.

_____. 1981. "Comment on: 'Sacred Cows and Water Buffalo in India,' by S. A. Freed and R. S. Freed." *Current Anthropology* 22:498.

_____. 1982. "Comment on: 'Bovine Sex and Species Ratios in India,' by A. Vaidyanathan et al." *Current Anthropology* 23:379–380.

Ross, Eric B., 1980. "Introduction." In *Beyond the Myths of Culture: Essays in Cultural Materialism.* Eric B. Ross, ed., pp. xix–xxix. New York: Academic Press.

Rossi, Ino, 1974. "Structuralism as Scientific Method." In *The Unconscious in Culture: The Structuralism of Claude Levi-Strauss.* Ino Rossi, ed., pp. 60–106. New York: Dutton.

Rynkiewich, Michael A., and James P. Spradley, 1976. *Ethics and Anthropology: Dilemmas in Fieldwork.* New York: John Wiley.

Sahlins, Marshall, 1976a. *The Use and Abuse of Biology: An Anthropological Critique of Sociobiology.* Ann Arbor: University of Michigan Press.

_____. 1976b. *Culture and Practical Reason.* Chicago: University of Chicago Press.

Salmon, Merrilee H., 1982. *Philosophy and Archaeology.* New York: Academic Press.

Salzman, Philip Carl, 1986. "Is Traditional Fieldwork Outmoded?" *Current Anthropology,* 27 (5):528–530.

Sarbin, Theodore R., 1969. "The Scientific Status of the Mental Illness Metaphor." In *Changing Perspectives in Mental Illness.* Stanley C. Plog and Robert B. Edgerton, eds., pp. 9–31. New York: Holt, Rinehart and Winston.

Schmidt, Wilhelm, 1939. *The Culture Historical Method of Ethnology.* New York: Fortuny.

Schneider, David, 1968. *American Kinship: A Cultural Account.* Englewood Cliffs, N.J.: Prentice-Hall.

Scholte, Bob, 1966. "Epistemic Paradigms: Some Problems in Cross-cultural Research on Social Anthropological History and Theory." *American Anthropologist* 68:1192–1201.

_____. 1972. "Toward a Reflexive and Critical Anthropology." In *Reinventing Anthropology.* Dell Hymes, ed., pp. 430–457. New York: Random House.

————. 1973. "The Structural Anthropology of Claude Levi-Strauss." In *Handbook of Social and Cultural Anthropology.* John J. Honingmann, ed., pp. 637–716. Chicago: Rand McNally.

————. 1980. "Anthropological Traditions: Their Definition." In *Anthropology: Ancestors and Heirs.* Stanley Diamond, ed., pp. 53–87. The Hague: Mouton.

————. 1984a. "Reason and Culture: The Universal and the Particular Revisited." *American Anthropologist,* 86 (4):960–965.

————. 1984b. "On Geertz's Interpretive Theoretical Program." *Current Anthropology,* 25 (4):540–542.

Schutz, Alfred, 1967. *The Phenomenology of the Social World.* Evanston, Ill.: Northwestern University Press.

Schwabe, Calvin W., 1979. "Comment on: 'Questions in the Sacred Cow Controversy,' by F. J. Simoons." *Current Anthropology* 20:488–489.

Schwartzberg, Joseph E., 1979. "Comment on: 'Questions in the Sacred Cow Controversy,' by F. J. Simoons." *Current Anthropology* 20:489.

Shankman, Paul, 1984. "The Thick and the Thin: On the Interpretive Theoretical Program of Clifford Geertz." *Current Anthropology* 25:261–279.

Sheehy, Gail, 1976. *Passages: The Predictable Crises of Adult Life.* New York: Dutton.

Shweder, Richard A., and Robert A. LeVine, eds., 1984. *Culture Theory: Essays on Mind, Self, and Emotion.* Cambridge: Cambridge University Press.

Silverman, Sydel, ed., 1981. *Totems and Teachers: Perspectives on the History of Anthropology.* New York: Columbia University Press.

Simoons, Frederick J., 1979. "Questions in the Sacred Cow Controversy." *Current Anthropology* 20:467–493.

Spindler, George D., ed., 1978. *The Making of Psychological Anthropology.* Berkeley: University of California Press.

Spindler, George, and Louise Spindler, 1983. "Anthropologists View American Culture." In *Annual Reviews in Anthropology* 12:49–78. Palo Alto, Calif.: Annual Reviews.

Srivastava, Vinay, and S. L. Malik, 1982. "On Ethnography and the Sacred Cow Controversy." *Current Anthropology* 22:222–223.

Stevens-Long, Judith, 1979. *Adult Life: Developmental Processes.* Palo Alto, Calif.: Mayfield Publishing.

Stevenson, Joanne Sabol, 1977. *Issues and Crises During Middlescence.* New York: Appleton-Century-Crofts.

Steward, Julian, 1955. *Theory of Culture Change: The Methodology of Multilinear Evolution.* Urbana: University of Illinois Press.

Sturtevant, William C., 1964. "Studies in Ethnoscience." *American Anthropologist* 66 (3):99–131.

Suttles, Wayne, 1966. "Comment on: 'The Cultural Ecology of India's Sacred Cattle,' by Marvin Harris." *Current Anthropology* 7:63.

Szasz, Thomas, 1961. *The Myth of Mental Illness.* New York: Harper and Row.

————. 1963. *Law, Liberty, and Psychiatry: An Inquiry into the Social Uses of Mental Health Practices.* New York: Macmillan.

————. 1978. *The Myth of Psychotherapy: Mental Health as Religion, Rhetoric, and Repression.* Garden City, N.Y.: Anchor Press/Doubleday.

Thoresen, Timothy H.H., ed., 1975. *Toward a Science of Man: Essays in the History of Anthropology.* The Hague: Mouton.

Turner, Victor, 1969. *The Ritual Process.* Chicago: Aldine Publishing.

————. 1974. *Dramas, Fields, and Metaphors.* Ithaca, N.Y.: Cornell University Press.

Turner, Victor W., and Edward M. Bruner, eds., 1986. *The Anthropology of Experience.* Urbana: University of Illinois Press.

Tyler, Stephen A., ed., 1969. *Cognitive Anthropology.* New York: Holt, Rinehart and Winston.

Tylor, Edward B., 1971. *Primitive Culture: Researches into the Development of Mythology, Philosophy, Religion, Language, Art and Custom.* London: J. Murray.

————. 1973. "Primitive Culture." In *High Points in Anthropology.* Paul Bohannan and Mark Glazer, eds., pp. 63–78. New York: Alfred A. Knopf.

Ulin, Robert C., 1984. *Understanding Cultures: Perspectives in Anthropology and Social Theory.* Austin: University of Texas Press.

Vaidyanathan, A., K. N. Nair, and Marvin Harris, 1982. "Bovine Sex and Species Ratios in India." *Current Anthropology* 23:365–383.

Van Gennep, Arnold, 1960. *The Rites of Passage.* Chicago: University of Chicago Press (originally published 1909).

Varenne, Hervé, ed., 1986. *Symbolizing America.* Lincoln: University of Nebraska Press.

Vayda, Andrew P., 1966. "Comment on: 'The Cultural Ecology of India's Sacred Cattle,' by Marvin Harris." *Current Anthropology* 7:63.

Voget, Fred W., 1975. *A History of Ethnology.* New York: Holt, Rinehart and Winston.

Wagley, Charles, 1977. *Welcome of Tears: The Tapirapé Indians of Central Brazil.* New York: Oxford University Press.

Wallace, Anthony F. C., 1966. *Religion: An Anthropological View.* Homewood, Ill.: Dorsey Press.

————. 1972. "Mental Illness, Biology, and Culture." In *Psychological Anthropology.* Francis L.K. Hsu, ed., pp. 255–295. Cambridge, Mass.: Schenkman Publishing.

Watson, Patty Jo, Steven A. LeBlanc, and Charles L. Redman, 1971. *Explanation in Archeology: An Explicitly Scientific Approach.* New York: Columbia University Press.

————. 1974. "The Covering Law Model in Archaeology: Practical Uses and Formal Interpretations." *World Archaeology* 6:125–132.

Werner, Oswald, 1973. "Structural Anthropology." In *Main Currents in Cultural Anthropology.* Raoul Naroll and Frada Naroll, eds., pp. 281–307. Englewood Cliffs, N.J.: Prentice-Hall.

Westen, Drew, 1984. "Cultural Materialism: Food for Thought or Bum Steer?" *Current Anthropology,* 25 (5):639–653.

White, Leslie, 1949. *The Science of Culture.* New York: Farrar, Straus.

————. 1954. "Review of *Culture: A Critical Review of Concepts and Definitions* by A. L. Kroeber and C. Kluckhohn." *American Anthropologist* 56:461–486.

————. 1959. *The Evolution of Culture.* New York: McGraw-Hill.

Willey, Gordon R., and Jeremy Sabloff, 1974. *A History of American Archaeology.* San Francisco: W. H. Freeman.

Wilson, Edward O., 1975. *Sociobiology: The New Synthesis.* Cambridge, Mass.: Harvard University Press.

Winch, Peter, 1958. *The Idea of a Social Science and Its Relation to Philosophy.* London: Routledge and Paul.

Wissler, Clark, 1917. *The American Indian.* New York: D. C. McMurtrie.

Wolf, Eric R., 1964. *Anthropology.* Englewood Cliffs, N.J.: Prentice-Hall.

Index